THE PROMISE OF REINHOLD NIEBUHR

THE PROMISE OF
REINHOLD NIEBUHR

Third Edition

Gabriel Fackre

William B. Eerdmans Publishing Company
Grand Rapids, Michigan / Cambridge, U.K.

First edition © 1970 by Gabriel Fackre; published by J. B. Lippincott Company
Second edition © 1994 by University Press of America, Inc.

Third edition published 2011 by
Wm. B. Eerdmans Publishing Co.
2140 Oak Industrial Drive N.E., Grand Rapids, Michigan 49505 /
P.O. Box 163, Cambridge CB3 9PU U.K.

Printed in the United States of America

17 16 15 14 13 12 11   7 6 5 4 3 2 1

Library of Congress Cataloging-in-Publication Data

Fackre, Gabriel J.
The promise of Reinhold Niebuhr / Gabriel Fackre. — 3rd ed.
p.   cm.
Includes bibliographical references.
ISBN 978-0-8028-6610-3 (pbk.: alk. paper)
1. Niebuhr, Reinhold, 1892-1971.   I. Title.

BX4827.N5F3   2011
230'.044092 — dc22

2010046341

www.eerdmans.com

To

James Luther Adams

Contents

Contents

Contents

Foreword to the First Edition

No native-born American more readily became a candidate
for inclusion in this series of books on futures [*The Promise of Theology*, 11 vols., Martin E. Marty, general editor, Lippincott, 1969-71] than did Reinhold Niebuhr. For over a third of a
century he has been a shaping influence in theology, social ethics,
and public policy. Those who speak in faintly condescending
tones about other twentieth-century giants in religious thought,
as if their days are past and their contributions forgotten, are
more reluctant to do so when Niebuhr's name is brought up.

For one thing, the longtime Union Theological Seminary professor is a moving target. As both his biographer and Professor
Fackre have pointed out, he has always had "the courage to
change." Today's radicals cannot dismiss a man who so early saw
prospects in Marxian thought. The people on the New Politics
part of the spectrum cannot deny that he helped set a basis for
them in his Christian realism. Mainline theologians applaud the
way in which he was grounded in classical Christian themes, not
even shunning some unpopular doctrines like "original sin." And
even innocent bystanders live with policies developed by men
who acknowledge that Niebuhr's thought informed theirs.

Foreword to the First Edition

Niebuhr has his enemies, too — another good sign that there is potency and promise in his thought.

Like most of the subjects of books in this series, Niebuhr has been a very productive man. Unlike many of them, he has not ordinarily chosen the systematic tome as the means of expressing himself — though *The Nature and Destiny of Man* towers in that category. To approach Niebuhr one must read thousands of editorials and short articles, cope with impressive sermons, tie together themes from many short occasional books. Fackre has done this and presents readers with a coherent view of Niebuhr, accenting the themes that now have to be wrestled with more than others, themes which suggest some directions theology and Christian action could well take today.

MARTIN E. MARTY
The University of Chicago

Foreword to the Revised Edition

—— ⊗∞⊗ ——

In the republication of this "small work," as the author calls it, is a convergence of scattered events in my lifetime: the early summer camp friendship of two teenaged boys, the discovery in my parish ministry of this text that enhanced lay discussion of ethics/theology, and the reunion in Andover Newton Theological School where I transposed the parish experience into a course that bridges parish practice and the systematic theology that Gabriel Fackre teaches. *The Promise of Reinhold Niebuhr* is still, as it was two decades ago, the best introduction to the sense of Reinhold Niebuhr's committed life and substantial thought.

Here is a book that gives handles for setting up study about a figure of our century, much as the handles gave my awkward arms purchase on the mattresses I was instructed to move from cottage to cottage in the long-ago summer camp. I look backward now at the handles that made life's meaning accessible; how important to an unwieldy job those grippers are. To many students now in seminary, theology is unwieldy, a different load of material that they often grasp and hug, as bulky mattresses are held, in the hope that proximity and earnestness will somehow make the top-

ics useful. Handles change the work from sheer effort to orga-
nized expectancy.

From camp to parish to seminary was a journey both Gabe and
I took without seeing each other in the meantime. I had, also, a
short journey with RN during Union Seminary student years in
the forties. References about Reinie in recent books refer to his
concern for students and his never-neglectful attention to
coursework. Amidst all his travels, his classes were met and his individual students, known. I knew that in this way: Reinie recognized my name as Czech and remembered having met my father
as a representative of Church World Service in Europe. Putting
together his political curiosity — indeed, anxiety — about central Europe and his intuition that my father's absence made my final school year one of turbulence and decision-making, he always
stopped me if only for a moment to ask about Dad and about me.
He was interested; he was a pastor. His momentary and impressive example taught me the lesson of my ministry: that it *is* possible to be a pastor and continue to study, that pondering is a theological task for the parish.

In *The Promise of Reinhold Niebuhr* Gabe has given well-
crafted handles to Niebuhr's place in twentieth-century theology.
He has RN's center of gravity in the seminary and church, not the
university; his freedom from "captivity to the givens"; and his
"dialectical dreaming" toward hope. Indeed, Gabe, too, moves
within the life of the church from parish to seminary.

Parishioners and students always push the theological point
towards practice in daily life. They must; we must. Crucial then is
the work of RN regarding the dialectic of love and justice. Jesus'
absolute injunction to love, the ultimate "impossible possibility,"
is a goad to faith and often the stumbling-block that hurls humans into the practical impasse. An environmental engineer says,
"I know what it means to love the planet in a perfect sense. Each

day I meet hindrances that negate every effort to honor and care for God's creation. So my prayer each night is 'God, I've failed . . . again.' How long can I endure being judged by the standard of perfection?"

In such a dilemma, Niebuhr spoke of justice. Love commonly means the self's active care for another. Justice commonly means the consideration of all parties without special interest or personal preference. Niebuhr maintained that love is under obligation to accept the best principles it can for the ordering of society. Justice as one such principle cannot be repealed by love. It is the mediating principle between absolute love and the power principles of society; it is the relative embodiment of love in social situations.

Niebuhr's realistic approach takes into account the human tendency to think highly of self. Modern culture too easily assumes that a level of empathy, indeed sanctification, is a simple possibility. But the more seriously the imperative to love is taken, the more vulnerable are we to "crash." With our engineer, it is easy to be pessimistic, even defeated, when out of the imperative to love, our effort for good loses. RN interposes justice. Love, he said, can always raise justice to new heights, but love in its redemptive and creative freedom is at times hazardous for society precisely because it values freedom so much more than it values order. So, he says, seek justice first, keeping both love and justice in tension. He is content with neither a transcendence which neglects the world nor with an immanence which neglects God. He makes each the critic of the other, keeping the obligation to establish "indeterminate degrees" of justice.

What saves such an analysis from cold logic are two qualities Gabe catches in Reinie's faith: humor/irony and piety. Through the toughest talk and the densest debate shone the irony of the historical situation and the humor of the personal dilemma. Besides, RN was a pious man. He was formed by the rigors of Reformed obligation and the sanctity of Anglican liturgy. Living with uncertainty, he was clear; touched by many lives and cultures, he remained a lone figure within the narrow fold of a sustaining family.

Giving a place to justice as the proximate exhibition of love, and to ambiguity as hope for perfection, has rescued many contemporary students who ask the engineer's question. Not intended as a practical reply, and certainly not as an answer to answerless questions, Niebuhr's dialectic is a handle that facilitates present theological debate. Fackre's little book keeps before us this point of present relevance.

DANIEL NOVOTNY

Preface to the Third Edition

❦

Who are the theologians of promise today? So asked Martin E. Marty in his "Promise" series some forty years ago.[1] This book is about one of those theologians, who, among some others, has stood the test of time. I am pleased to have written the 1970 volume on the durable Reinhold Niebuhr. This is a third issuing of that work, with some updating of the 1994 revised edition that appeared in the context, even then, of renewed interest in him.

What better sign of these particular times of crushed expectations and mordant forecasts than evidence of fresh attention to Reinhold Niebuhr and the kind of response he made, in his own era, to comparable illusions and despairs? An example of this new interest is a recent collection of essays by leading theologians, historians, and ethicists who describe him as an "American original."[2] One refrain in that work is the timeliness of his views on matters political in the first decade of the twenty-first century.

1. Martin E. Marty, gen. ed., *The Promise of Theology*, 11 vols. (Philadelphia: Lippincott, 1969-71).

2. Daniel F. Rice, ed., *Reinhold Niebuhr Revisited: Engagements with an American Original* (Grand Rapids: Wm. B. Eerdmans Pub. Co., 2009).

Consider President Barack Obama's testimony to his debt to Niebuhr.[3] Indeed, as in previous eras, folk at both ends of the spectrum pay tribute to him. See neo-conservative David Brooks's *New York Times* column of April 26, 2007.[4] Important, as well, is a 2006 essay by Peter Beinart.[5] And then there is the December 1, 2009, *Christian Century* piece by Andrew Finstuen, "Where Is Reinhold Niebuhr When We Need Him?: This American Mess."[6] For a searching application of Niebuhrian thought to recent American foreign policy and actions, see also Andrew Bacevich's *The Limits of Power: The End of American Exceptionalism.*[7] Does this renewed attention put into question the comment of Arthur Schlesinger Jr. in his 2005 article, "Forgetting Reinhold Niebuhr"?[8] The lamentation itself illustrates his continuing significance, since Schlesinger was one of numerous "Atheists for Niebuhr." But it is not only politics that invites another look at this giant. The recent book by Niebuhr's daughter, Elisabeth Sifton, on the "serenity prayer"[9] reflects his impor-

3. See, for example, "Obama's Theologian," broadcast on *Speaking of Faith* with Krista Tippett (Feb. 2009) and archived at http://being.publicradio.org/programs/2009/obamas-theologian/. See also, Brian Urquat, "What You Can Learn from Reinhold Niebuhr," *New York Review of Books,* March 26, 2009, 32.

4. "Obama, Gospel and Verse," *New York Times,* April 26, 2007, A25.

5. "The Rehabilitation of a Cold-War Liberal," *The New York Times Magazine,* April 30, 2006, 40-45.

6. *The Christian Century,* Vol. 126, No. 24 (December 1, 2008), 11-12. In the same issue editor John Buchanan pays tribute to him in an editorial, "The Niebuhr Connection" (p. 3).

7. (Henry Holt and Company, 2008). Note his unusual tribute to Niebuhr: "Writing decades ago, Reinhold Niebuhr anticipated that predicament [America's "three interlocking crises" — economic/cultural, political, and military] with uncanny accuracy and astonishing prescience. As such, perhaps more than any figure in our recent history, he may help us discern a way out" (p. 6).

8. *The New York Times Book Review,* September 18, 2005.

9. Elisabeth Sifton, *The Serenity Prayer: Faith and Politics in a Time of Peace*

tance in piety and theology, as does continuing interest in his Gifford Lectures.

What is it about this theologian that makes Niebuhr a thinker of "promise" for the president? His appreciation of Niebuhr may go back to Obama's earlier days as a community organizer on Chicago's South Side. Saul Alinsky, the inspiration and interpreter of the community organization movement, regarded Niebuhr as one of his mentors and may have led the president to Niebuhr's works.[10] My speculations here are based not only on learning from Alinsky's *Reveille for Radicals* and *Rules for Radicals* but on hearing him lecture in a University of Chicago Divinity School class in the late 1940s. They are further bolstered by my stint as pastor of a congregation/settlement house in Bridgeport, a South Side Chicago community adjacent to the Back of the Yards district where Alinsky honed his skills in community

---

and War (New York: W. W. Norton & Co., 2003). After a recent much-publicized claim that the prayer was not composed by Niebuhr (following a history of such claims), a Religion News Service story in the December 29, 2009, *Christian Century,* "Scholar alters view, says Niebuhr probably wrote 'Serenity Prayer,'" reports a 1937 source citing a Niebuhr prayer: "Father give us courage to change what must be altered, serenity to accept what cannot be helped, and the insight to know one from the other" (p. 15).

10. In an observation by Jerry Kellman, an associate of Obama's in his community organizing days, both Obama's debt to Alinsky and his critique of him come clear: "There is a machismo which makes organizers afraid to admit that they are moved by ideals rather than self-interest. But most of what we do in life is, of course, a combination of both. Barack understood this, and so did I, and so Alinsky's teaching on self-interest was balanced by Dr. King's appeal to our mutuality." In David Remnick, *The Bridge: The Life and Rise of Barack Obama* (New York: Alfred A. Knopf, 2010), p. 164. On the larger matters of ultimate commitment, see Obama's insightful discussion of the current religious landscape and his own basic convictions in the chapter "Faith" in *The Audacity of Hope: Thoughts on Reclaiming the American Dream* (New York: Crown Publishers, 2006), 195-226.

organization. Alinsky was a passionate reformer who believed that social change happens when appeal is made to the self-interest of the underdog, rather than relying on preachments to the powerful. He sought to develop coalitions of the aggrieved — including groups that often were pitted against one another — in the struggle against common afflictions. A doctrine of human nature operates in these assumptions and strategies. We are all "sinners," although Alinsky did not use these biblical terms. Self-interest is, therefore, a crucial factor in organizing the powerless in the quest for justice. And it means that the hubris of the powerful can be challenged only when the powerless organize to check it. At work here is the realism that Niebuhr espoused. And, like Niebuhr, Alinsky blended his realism with a vision of a world of human flourishing.

Obama, the "visionary realist," demonstrated that difficult mix in his lecture upon receipt of the Nobel Peace Prize in 2009. Jeff Zeleny caught this creative tension in his report of the event, commenting that "He delivered a mix of realism and idealism, implicitly criticizing both the Rev. Dr. Martin Luther King as naïve about a dangerous world and President George W. Bush as too quick to set aside fundamental American values in pursuit of security."[11] The "implicitly" should be unpacked. The president reveres King. Obama, however, observed here and many times elsewhere that the responsibilities of a head of state are not the same as those of someone who heads a movement, such as King and Gandhi.[12] The president is reflecting a theme illustrated by sociologist Robert Hoover's bell curve. Hoover argues that effective social change happens when a small cadre of "innovators"

11. Jeff Zeleny, "Accepting Peace Prize, Obama Offers 'Hard Truth,'" *The New York Times,* December 11, 2009, A17.
12. So described by Remnick, *The Bridge,* 348.

have their cause taken up by a larger group of "early adopters" who, in turn, bring aboard the yet larger company of "early majoritarians." Such a coalition, he contends, reaches the tipping point of the sought-for change.[13] Not a few later commentators saw this visionary realism as "Niebuhrian."

While the biblical "vision" is a radical norm — for Niebuhr it was the Kingdom of God in its purity at the End of history — for Alinsky and Obama it would be a utopian hope of social transformation (perhaps for believer Obama, it also would be that Kingdom); a romantic expectation that it will be achieved in this world is given up. Rather, the vision functions as a lure toward higher approximations and a judge of lower ones. Thus, as the president has said, be wary of "emotional absolutism"[14] and remember that "the perfect can be the enemy of the good." The good has to do with a maximum feasible goal in a particular circumstance in this world of competing self-interests that plague history to the End. Often that means that the visionary realist will find himself or herself opposed or misunderstood, on one hand, by the visionary who assumes that the perfect is possible, and, on the other, by the simplistic realist whose goals are too pragmatic or captive to the givens. Of course, the one who seeks to blend vision and reality is not exempt from the temptation to sacrifice one value for the sake of the other.[15] Stay tuned as we watch the president walk this tight-rope. Chapter 4 of this book attempts to show how Niebuhr negotiated this difficult transit.

13. Robert Hoover, "Empirically Tested Categories of Normative Adopters," Figure 6, mimeograph, 1971, referencing data in Everett Rogers, *Diffusion of Innovation* (New York: Free Press, 1962).

14. Remnick, *The Bridge,* 430.

15. The brilliant biography by David Remnick, *The Bridge,* while essentially a narrative, demonstrates throughout the quest by Obama to hold together passionate ideals in tension with political realities.

In a searching critique of current ways of Christian encounter with culture along with his alternative proposal, James Davison Hunter strikes just these Niebuhrian notes: "What this means is that faithful Christian witness is fated to exist in the tension between the historical and the transcendent; between the social realities that press on human existence and the spiritual and ethical requirements of the gospel; between the morality of the society in which Christian believers live and the will of God."[16]

An irony attends the current interest in Alinsky. Niebuhr, with his own appreciation for irony, namely *The Irony of American History,* would be among the first to discern it. Dick Armey, fierce critic of Obama, is said to have learned from Alinsky how to mount grassroots protests against the president's policies. This produced the August 2009 display of raucous outbursts by attendees at many town meetings held by members of Congress, magnified by the 24/7 news cycle on cable TV. This also led to the protest signs and shouts of "liar" and worse at a massive September 12 "tea party" demonstration that year in Washington engineered by Armey's organization and those of like mind. One must ask, however, whether the pretended realism in the methods and goals of these protests has not morphed into cynicism. The dictum holds true that "where there is no vision the people perish." If those who have discovered in our midst a stewardship of that vision in company with a sobriety about hoped-for outcomes are right, then "Reinie" does seem to be around just when we need him.

This third edition of *The Promise of Reinhold Niebuhr,* appearing thirty years after the first, prompts, in conclusion, some more personal observations. They are interlaced with ties and debts to

16. *To Change the World: The Irony, Tragedy, and Possibility of Christianity in the Late Modern World* (Oxford: Oxford University Press, 2010), p. 183. See especially chapter 7.

another mentor, James Luther Adams. I first came to Niebuhr by way of Adams.

While I was a first-year student at the University of Chicago, I took a required course in "constructive theology" taught by Professor Adams. One of the readings was Niebuhr's two-volume Gifford Lectures, *The Nature and Destiny of Man*. In my struggle with the pervasive "neo-naturalist" theology of Henry Nelson Wieman, who taught at that time in the University's Divinity School, I discovered in Niebuhr a point of view with strong social justice accents and fresh and persuasive biblical warrants. My first paper in theology, with not a few citations from Niebuhr, was graded, however, with a B+ over D, the latter a wake-up call by Adams for "style."

In that same term, Reinhold Niebuhr appeared on the Chicago campus for a preaching engagement at the University's Rockefeller Chapel. In connection with it, Adams hosted a dialogue with Niebuhr in Meadville House, a student residence in which I happened to be living. What an event! The two engaged in an animated theological-cum-political back-and-forth while a roomful of us listened entranced and entered with trepidation from time to time into the conversation.

During his stay at the University that week, a luncheon was arranged for Niebuhr at the Quadrangle Club so that he might meet with Chicago-area theologians. I was a student waiter at this faculty dining club. The hostess, knowing of my Divinity School connection, assigned me to serve the group in the Club's private dining room. During the discharge of my duties as waiter I was able to overhear yet another lively exchange. My clearest memory is of Joseph Hartounian, a well-known figure from McCormick Seminary, then on the city's North Side, sitting next to his friend "Reinie," with both theologians in animated conversation about our "human nature and destiny." (Not long after that, my cordial

relations with the Club management ended, as another Meadville resident and I led a noon walk-out of the seventeen student
waiters and waitresses in protest of the defeat of an amendment
to the Club rules that would have eliminated the blackball practice that occasioned a racial, gender, and political discrimination
charged by its proponents. Professor Adams was our adviser in
the action, and, no doubt, the shadow of Niebuhr could have
been seen by a discerning eye.)[17]
My next contact with Niebuhr came while working on a B.D.
thesis under the supervision of Adams, "Religious Representation and Reality in the Thought of Reinhold Niebuhr." The leading issue, discussed against the background of the neo-naturalism
of Wieman, was whether Niebuhr's thought on myth was itself a
kind of closet naturalism. Indeed, Wieman judged that to be the
case in a course I took with him in his last year at the Divinity
School. I wrote to Niebuhr at Union Seminary:

> I am writing my B.D. thesis on the problem of myth and
> truth in relation to your concept of God (with respect to the
> traditions of psychologism, sociologism, idealism, and dialec-
> tical theology). . . . I can appreciate the remark that "all theol-
> ogy is mythology," but does that preclude metaphysical state-
> ments about the nature of God? . . . Should not some
> distinctions be made between better and worse definitions?
> The problem becomes particularly acute when all shades of
> naturalism and supernaturalism ascribe their own ontologi-
> cal notions to your idea of God. . . .[18]

17. See "Student Waiters Strike at U. of C.," *Chicago Sun*, June 17, 1945;
"Quit U. of C. club; charge racial bias," *Chicago Daily Times;* and Emily Kadens,
The Quadrangle Club 1893-1993: Creating a Sense of Society (Chicago: Quadrangle Club, 1993), 68, 70, 77.
18. Letter from Gabriel Fackre to Reinhold Niebuhr, fall 1947, The Gabriel

Niebuhr replied in an October 29, 1947, letter. Among other things he wrote:

> I completely agree with you that distinctions between better and worse definitions of God should be made, and I have constantly made them. There is, for example, no warrant for anyone assuming that my definitions are naturalistic, for I have rejected naturalistic definitions on almost every page of my work. . . . Professor Wieman is quite wrong in suggesting that myth is used in order to evade metaphysical distinctions. It is used rather to do justice to the complexity of the relation between the eternal ground of history and the flow of events in history.[19]

What better support of the main theme of a novice's B.D thesis? Interestingly, the issue of Niebuhr's "naturalism" has continued to the present. So to this edition of the book I have added Chapter 7, which is a response to the criticism of Niebuhr by Stanley Hauerwas in his own Gifford Lectures.[20]

Nineteen forty-eight marked another milestone in my journey with Niebuhr. My spouse, Dorothy, also a university student, and I were part of a "Summer Seminar in Europe," studying "The Church and the Workingclasses" and "British Christian Socialism." Through Professor Adams's contact with Niebuhr, we received names of several of Niebuhr's former students and present associates whom we then reached in our research efforts. Among

---

Fackre Manuscript Collection, Special Collections, Princeton Theological Seminary Libraries.

19. Letter from Reinhold Niebuhr to Gabriel Fackre, Oct. 29, 1947, Princeton Theological Seminary Libraries.

20. For a more detailed response to Hauerwas, see the file on Niebuhr and Hauerwas in the writings section of www.gabrielfackre.com.

them were Alexander Miller, Ronald Preston, Donald Baillie, and John MacMurray, as well George MacLeod, founder of the then worker/pastor Iona Community who welcomed us to the island. After our summer in Britain we took a boat to the Continent and then hitch-hiked to Amsterdam to attend, as wide-eyed students, the first assembly of the World Council of Churches. But, sadly, we just missed witnessing there the historic exchange between Niebuhr and Karl Barth.[21]

The following year we had yet another fortuitous encounter with Niebuhr. While serving Chicago's Back-of-the-Yards mission, Raymond Chapel, we learned that Niebuhr was to speak one evening at Orchestra Hall in downtown Chicago. Convinced that this was a rare opportunity for our parishioners, we took several carloads of them to the service. Niebuhr was at his riveting best, striding back and forth across the stage and letting fly one after another of his sometimes stratospheric theological asides. Out of the corner of my eye I watched one of the congregation's saints, Mrs. Ionone, who seemed entranced. Later, I asked her what she thought of the service. She remarked, "I didn't understand a word he said, but I do believe he had the Holy Spirit."

While serving in a two-point mission charge in the steel towns of Homestead and Duquesne, Pennsylvania, for a decade following graduation from Divinity School, my spouse and I faithfully read the journal Niebuhr founded, *Christianity and Crisis,* as well

---

21. Interpreting Barth's stress on the role of the church as preaching the one Word faithfully and calling the political powers to repentance, but not engaging directly in social action, Niebuhr declared in a major address to the assembly, "It is true . . . repentance is always required even as evil always flourishes. But it is wrong to preach this Gospel *sub specie aeternitatis* as if there were no history with its time and seasons." Niebuhr was too quick to dismiss Barth's thought as apolitical, for Barth did make political judgments, although not with the same use of secular resources that were part of Niebuhr's arsenal of analysis.

as devouring his later works, attempting to make connections between our Niebuhr-*cum*-Barth perspective and the challenges of industrial America, aware that in his own pastoral ministry in Detroit he had faced similar challenges in an earlier era. Then in the mid-sixties, moving from parish to seminary teaching, I began to write now and then for *Christianity and Crisis.* A version of one of these articles, "Realism and Vision," appears in this book. Coming to the close of this history of glancing contacts with Niebuhr, I was pleased to tell Martin Marty in 1969 that I'd write the small work on Niebuhr for his developing series on the promise of various theologians. I was very gratified, as well, to have that history capped by a note from Niebuhr himself, who had received from the press a copy of the first edition of this work and wrote on September 24, 1970, in this letter that I treasure:

> Thank you so much for your excellent book on my books. . . . For a man who lives in the last years of his life, "promise" is not exactly accurate, but the editors rather than you, are responsible for it. . . .[22]

Reinhold Niebuhr died in 1971.

PENTECOST 2010

---

22. Letter from Reinhold Niebuhr to Gabriel Fackre, Princeton Theological Seminary Libraries.

chapter 1

A PILGRIM ON THE WAY

———— ∞∞∞ ————

D uring his lifetime, North American graduate study had accepted more doctoral dissertations on the topic of Reinhold Niebuhr's theology than on any other twentieth-century theologian. Since then, books analyzing him, as well as retrospective notes by friends and colleagues, thicken card files. Though every crevice of his story seems to have been explored, this biographical chapter gives special attention to some qualities that mark Niebuhr's spiritual journey.

The Early Years

Karl Paul Reinhold Niebuhr was born in Wright City, Missouri, on June 21, 1892. His parents were serving a German-speaking congregation of the small Evangelical Synod, a denomination which mixed the Lutheran and Reformed traditions. The Reverend Gustav Niebuhr and his wife, Lydia, had other children — Helmut Richard, for some the "other Niebuhr," whom Reinhold always regarded as the better theologian; Hulda, a notable theologian, teacher, and writer affiliated for many years with McCormick Theological Seminary in Chicago; Walter, a pioneering publisher and businessman; and Hubert, who died in infancy. Pastor Niebuhr had left his homeland in protest of Prussian rigidities, and therefore, while discipline was not absent, a warmth of give-and-take were very much part of family life. Reinhold frequently expressed his gratitude for the security, love, and openness of those family years.

"Reinie" grew up in Missouri and Illinois parsonages. One day he announced that his father was "the most interesting man in town." It came as no surprise, therefore, that he moved toward the professional ministry, entering the Evangelical Synod's Elmhurst College in suburban Chicago, then going on to Eden Theological Seminary in Webster Groves, Missouri. His academic achievements and eagerness to break loose from the tight web of German church life pressed him to continue his studies at Yale where his keen mind carved out a respected niche for himself among the Ivy League sophisticates, and he earned a B.D. and an M.A. degree. The renowned exponent of evangelical liberalism, Douglas Clyde Macintosh, exercised a particularly strong influence on him, although during the Yale years and later professor and student had animated exchanges on their differences.

Strong commitment to the Evangelical Synod which had nourished and encouraged him and a certain fatigue with prolonged intellectual incubation led Niebuhr in 1915 to accept the pastorate of a small congregation in Detroit. His mother, alone since the death of his father in 1913, accompanied him to the new charge.

1915 to 1928: Detroit

Niebuhr launched his ministry in the company of the eighteen families of Bethel Evangelical Church, "the little German church around the corner." A Detroit population explosion, powerful preaching, and the dedicated organizational labors of Mrs. Lydia Niebuhr sent the membership to nearly seven hundred over the period of his thirteen-year ministry and put the congregation in an imposing new building. Reinhold later paid tribute to his mother's unofficial assistanceship which allowed him to be a peripatetic religious apologist particularly on secular podia across the nation. He also began his lifetime practice of writing the short, feisty journal article which soon brought animated retorts and lively debates.

In Detroit, Niebuhr began to face the realities of industrial America. His congregation was a cross-section of the metropolis, including a sprinkling of wage workers, a varied middle-class majority, and a few millionaires. His pastoral rounds and civic activities brought him in contact with the unemployed, with those retired at the height of their working powers because of the automobile industry's age policies, and with those suppliers and competitors in the industry who were broken by its giant — Ford. Henry Ford had a world reputation, not only as a technological innovator but also as a humanitarian who trailed behind him a well-publicized record of high wages, the five-day week, and employment of the handicapped.

It was in the closeup view of the human ravages left by big business that Niebuhr's social conscience and realism took form. Behind the "high wages" lay Henry Ford's high profits. And behind that was a production genius which included efficiency-engineered speedups, model changeover, retooling with its long factory shutdowns and mass layoffs, a Charlie Chaplin assembly-line life, the shelving of aged workers, and an anti-union policy. Niebuhr's response ran the gamut from personal ministry to public protest. He sought jobs for individual cast-offs; in the face of sharp protests by the Detroit Board of Commerce, he welcomed representatives of labor into his church forum groups to tell their story; to the vocal displeasure of Ford enterprises, he filed periodic reports with *The Christian Century* on the machinations of the automobile industry. This on-location exposure to the gap between the pretension and the performance of an industrial barony contributed to Niebuhr's realism, particularly regarding collectivities. Further, tirades initially directed at Ford developed into more sophisticated analyses of structural weaknesses in the economy that later took shape as an attack on capitalism.

Detroit was a laboratory in racial learning as well as in labor conflict. With the supply of European immigrants cut off by the war, the automobile industry drew large numbers of black citizens from the south. Niebuhr was among the church leaders who early participated in their struggle for basic justice, serving as the first chair of a Mayor's Commission on Racial Relations and taking controversial stands on specific issues of racial injustice. His congregation had a self-declared open membership policy and four or five African American families did attend services, though none joined.

Niebuhr's parish ministry spanned the period of the "Great War." He served as a member of a denominational commission that visited many of the stateside army camps and in 1919 with YMCA leader Sherwood Eddy he went on an inspection tour of Germany's Ruhr industrial valley, the reports of which stirred the U.S. government to take relief action. While going along initially with American participation in the war and expressing regrets to his Yale classmates at not being able to be a chaplain, Niebuhr became more and more disillusioned with that war and with war in general. In 1923 he became a declared pacifist and several years later was an active member of the Fellowship of Reconciliation (FOR).

Niebuhr's involvement in economic, social, and political affairs was influenced to no small extent by prophetic figures on the Detroit scene. One of them was Episcopal Bishop Charles Williams. While other clergy ran for cover in controversy, Williams consistently supported worker rights, justice for black citizens, and peace movements. He stood as proof to Niebuhr that the church could still produce an Amos. And, echoing Williams, he learned that in matters of social witness, the biblical position was often represented more faithfully by heirs of the prophets in the Jewish community, such as Detroit's Fred Butzell, than by followers of Christ in the church. This early comradeship with latter-day Amoses was to remain constant in Niebuhr's later political involvements and in his views on Jewish-Christian relations.

While the prophet's role figured prominently in Niebuhr's Detroit ministry, he was also a pastor attentive to the personal needs of his congregation. Both his own reflection in *Leaves from the Notebook of a Tamed Cynic* (1929) on the tragedies and joys of his parishioners, and their own testimony as well, reveal sensitivity to the claims of personal life and faithfulness to individual Christian ministrations. In later years Niebuhr expressed regret that in the midst of his busy public life he could not have given even more attention to the tender and intimate dimensions of ministry.

The association and friendship with Sherwood Eddy drew Niebuhr into the orbit of national life. Eddy opened the way to a larger audience by helping to provide funds for an assistant at Bethel Church so that the growing number of invitations to speak at colleges could be met. Thus began the circuit-riding that took Niebuhr to hundreds of centers of higher education in years to come. Plunging him further into the national arena was the request by social reformer Jane Addams to assist in the 1924 presidential campaign of Robert LaFollette. Meanwhile, Niebuhr was also writing for *The Atlantic Monthly* and *The Christian Century* (serving for a while on its editorial staff). In 1927 he wrote his first book, *Does Civilization Need Religion?*

As Niebuhr moved increasingly in circles beyond his local parish, the logic of a platform commensurate with this audience asserted itself. In 1928 he accepted a teaching post at Union Theological Seminary in New York City. Here he would be positioned at the crossroads of American intellectual and political ferment, where the traffic from European church life also flowed. These factors exercised a significant influence on the subsequent texture and tone of Niebuhr's life.

1929 to 1945: From Depression to Conflagration

Seminary life allowed, even demanded, more rigorous intellectual confrontation with the human issues than Niebuhr had encountered in Detroit. He read Karl Marx and came in touch with the currents of radical social criticism. On top of that were poured more data from the economic cataclysm of 1929 and its sequel, a hungry and despairing America. In the pages of *World Tomorrow,* an organ of the Fellowship of Reconciliation, and in such landmark volumes of the thirties as *Moral Man and Immoral Society* (1932), *Reflections on the End of an Era* (1934), and *An Interpretation of Christian Ethics* (1935), capitalism was pinpointed as the source of our social sickness and Roosevelt's New Deal was dismissed as a mild injection that dulled the patient's awareness of approaching death.

At the opening of the decade, Niebuhr further asserted his anticapitalist commitments as a leading spirit in founding the Fellowship of Socialist Christians and editing its periodical, *Radical Religion.* He joined the Socialist Party and in 1930 appeared on its ballot as a congressional candidate from a local New York district. He became a familiar figure in radical circles as he lived out his declaration to "move politically to the left and theologically to the right."

That latter mobility, "theologically to the right," distinguished him from many who had made the political journey leftward in the depressed thirties. The theological right meant a thread of biblical realism which wound itself into the socialist fabric. On the one hand, it forbade a mild social protest confident of a simple trust in human goodness, in the methods of moral suasion and education, and in history's steady escalation upward. On the other hand, it led him to reject the utopianism of the orthodox Marxist that claimed to have seen and secured the future and expressed itself in the fanaticism of a Stalinist purge or the mindless rigidity of the American Communist Party. For these reasons he was found regularly in the first ranks of antiestablishment activists who at the same time carried on a second front against Marxist ideologues seeking to gain control of reform movements. This double battle was waged in such groups as the New York Teachers' Union and other New York and national movements.

Toward the end of the decade, Niebuhr's attention turned more and more to the issues of war and peace. Having served for several years in earlier pacifist days as chair of the FOR, he now began to grapple with the Nazi phenomenon. The main lines of his criticism of pacifism were laid down in *An Interpretation of Christian Ethics*. As Hitler rattled German sabers more loudly, and as the horrible fate of the Jews broke into the consciousness of the world, Niebuhr became an outspoken critic of appeasement. He was by this time an international figure in both lecture and committee rooms and he had personal as well as political acquaintances in England and on the continent. Friendship with such expatriates as theologian Paul Tillich and social philosopher Eduard Heimann, and with leaders in the Christian resistance

7

movement like Dietrich Bonhoeffer, brought home to him the price being paid by inaction and dramatized, as well, the challenge to the church of the Nazis' "blood and soil" racism. While Niebuhr did not until 1941 plead radical intervention in terms of troops and a declaration of war, he backed many causes that aided refugees and supported the Allies materially, including the protection of cargo shipments.

As his antipacifist posture accelerated, so did his disengagement from the movements of another era whose commitments seemed obsolete. In 1940 Niebuhr resigned from the Socialist Party over its international policies and later helped to found the Liberal Party. While the Soviet bear and its American cubs gave off very ambiguous noises about the Nazis in this period, he took part in 1940 in the organization of the Union for Democratic Action (UDA) which sought to gather reformers around a common banner that excluded a doctrinaire Marxism.

All major political options were kept under critical review. The contest was among (1) a very imperfect form of Western democracy, (2) an all-out attack on the charter of human society itself (Nazism), and (3) a too-easy formulation of a new kind of humanism with demonic possibilities (Marxism). With these givens, Niebuhr was compelled to make the realignments cited above and more like them, often developing working relationships with those he had heretofore dismissed as captive to palliatives. For example, Eleanor Roosevelt, Elmer Davis, and others in left-wing Democratic Party activities became his close associates. Realignment brought with it access to the Luce publications and other major media. Although Niebuhr's still strong "politically to the left" leanings were hardly the company policy of *Life* and *Time,* his anti-Nazi posture and some of his theological insights were attractive to them. Moreover, the media could hardly ignore the position of a molder of international opinion.

Redirection also eventuated in a new association with government policy-makers, in particular in the State Department, whose public statements sometimes bore an almost embarrassing similarity to Niebuhrian concepts and language. In this period of changing loyalties and associations, many of his co-workers in the Fellowship of Christian Socialists followed him; the temperature change itself in this circle was signaled by an organizational nomenclature shift to the Frontier Fellowship and, finally, to Christian Action.

Niebuhr's extensive writing in this period included the astute political commentary of his early *Moral Man and Immoral Society,* then later essays in *The Nation, The New Republic, Harper's, Life,* and in his own publication, *Christianity and Crisis* (successor to *Radical Religion*); and probing theological analyses in media as varied as the editorial pages of the Evangelical and Reformed *Messenger* and the massively researched two-volume *The Nature and Destiny of Man* (1941, 1943). This latter classic was given as the 1939 Spring and Fall Term Gifford Lectures, against the backdrop of Edinburgh air raid sirens during the latter. Its statement of the Christian doctrine of humanity marked Niebuhr (despite his own disclaimers to be a theologian) as one of the most fertile theological minds of the twentieth century. Paralleling the more formal academic and political commentary was the continuing flow of sermons and addresses which found their way into such collections as *Beyond Tragedy* (1937) and *Discerning the Signs of the Times* (1946).

While the life of the mind and the struggle of nations occupied much of Niebuhr's attention during these years, time was made for tender things as well. He often remarked that without the latter there would have been few resources for the former. Vivacious Oxford honor student Ursula Keppel-Compton came to Union Seminary in the fall of 1930. Reinhold and she were married in 1931. The relationship had its intellectual electricity as well as its warm personal dimensions.[1] Ursula, demonstrating her own gifts as faculty member at Barnard College (ultimately heading the Department of Religion), proved to be one of the most astute critics of her husband's thought, influencing him significantly, as he testified in later years.

Born to Reinhold and Ursula were Christopher (1934) and Elisabeth, themselves lively participants in the warm family circle and remembered by Niebuhr in the dedication of *The Nature and Destiny of Man:* "to my wife Ursula who helped and to my children Christopher and Elisabeth who frequently interrupted me in the writing of these pages." The Niebuhr home also became a house of hospitality for students who looked forward to the once-a-week evening living-room dialogues. A number of strong friendships between the Niebuhrs and such intellectual and religious leaders as Will Herberg, Bishop William Scarlett, and others also flowered in the more private circle of Niebuhrian life.

The familial is not often recognized as an important ingredient in the prophetic. Neither is the devotional. Yet it was out of Niebuhrian spirituality that on a summer Sunday in 1942 (printed in 1943) a prayer took form that was destined to be used by chaplains and sufferers in countless hospital rooms and on battlefields, then adopted as the official prayer of Alcoholics Anonymous. "O God, give us serenity to accept what cannot be changed, courage to change what should be changed, and wisdom to distinguish the one from the other." While rarely vocal on a subject scarred by sentimentality, Niebuhr knew as a working pastor, and later as a weary man in the feverish thirties and forties when exhaustion from overwork felled him at several critical

1. See Ursula M. Niebuhr, *Remembering Reinhold Niebuhr* (New York: Harper Collins, 1991).

junctures, something of the sustenance and celebration that comes in "friendship with God."[2]

1945 to 1960: The Postwar Years

Niebuhr's reorientation towards working within the framework of major political options was crystallized in 1947 when he helped to form Americans for Democratic Action, a more broad-based outgrowth from UDA, independent in its party commitments but, in effect, a left-wing gadfly within the Democratic Party. With its non-Communist declaration, it distinguished itself from such parallel developments as the Progressive Citizens of America which supported the Henry Wallace presidential candidacy in 1948. This experience, and his growing stature as a political philosopher, drew Niebuhr further into the orbit of major American leadership as a consultant. The list of those who later sponsored at Union Seminary a social ethics chair bearing his name is an index of that influence. It included Adolph Berle, Chester Bowles, Ralph Bunche, David Dubinsky, William Hocking, Paul Hoffman, Hubert Humphrey, Robert Hutchins, Stanley Isaacs, George Kennan, Herbert Lehman, Walter Lippmann, Henry Luce, Robert Oppenheimer, Joseph Rauh, Walter Reuther, Eleanor Roosevelt, Beardsley Ruml, Arthur Schlesinger Jr., George Shuster, Adlai Stevenson, Charles Taft, and Norman Thomas. Overseas figures numbered in this group were W. H. Auden, President of the United Nations Charles Malik, Jacques Maritain, Sir Walter Moberly, Alan Paton, Sir Sarvepalli Radhakrishnan, Arnold Toynbee, and Barbara Ward.

2. For a collection of Reinhold's prayers and sermons, see Reinhold Niebuhr, *Justice and Mercy,* ed. Ursula M. Niebuhr (New York: Harper & Row, 1974 and Louisville: Westminster/John Knox Press, 1991).

Balancing the secular involvements were Niebuhr's associations in world Christianity. In 1937 at Oxford he had taken an active part in the ecumenical conversations on the relation of church to society. In 1948 he played a further role at the first assembly of the World Council of Churches in Amsterdam, writing resource material and providing sectional leadership. He also exchanged literary volleys with Karl Barth about the Council theme on the Lordship of Christ, defending its quest for solutions to the intricate problems of the day against allegations that such efforts represent Atlas-like pretentions. Having been on the wartime commission of the National Council of Churches "to establish a just and lasting peace," Niebuhr continued to serve as consultant to the Council on current events, working with (and not infrequently in opposition to) Secretary of State John Foster Dulles.

In the postwar period of ecclesiastical expansionism, peace-of-mind cults, and popular piety, Niebuhr questioned what he viewed as "cheap grace" (Dietrich Bonhoeffer's words) in the introversion of the religious establishment and the formulas of Billy Graham and Norman Vincent Peale. Although his sharpest barbs were reserved for church leaders, his attack on secular delusions never relented. For example, he saw in Alfred Kinsey and his widely publicized research on sexual response an illustration of naturalistic presuppositions about humanity (the equation of human sexuality with orgasm) which skewed his findings and gave less than reliable guidance for dealing with a strong biological impulse that in human beings is uniquely interwoven with subtler dimensions of personhood.

Some of those criticized by Niebuhr declined to engage in direct debate (Graham, Kinsey, Erich Fromm), but a lively give-and-take with others did go on in the pages of ecclesiastical and secular journals. Niebuhr acknowledged that a shift in his own thinking began to take place as a result of these dialogues and other influences. Feeling that a heavy use of biblical symbols was an impediment to interpreting the "truth in the myth," he increasingly sought more universal language, speaking of the doctrine of original sin more as our "self-regarding" propensity. Associated with this was the general softening of his former "homiletical polemics" against modern culture and a growing attempt to discern the traces of creativity in it and in human relationships in general. He never ceased, of course, to pinpoint the ambiguities and idolatries which pervade human experience. While continuing to take his own stand in the mainstream Reformation tradition, Niebuhr stressed with growing vigor the contributions of other religious traditions. Always affirmative of prophetic Judaism, he went further in the fifties to declare that the church should not attempt to convert Jews to the Christian faith, but rather should concentrate on a penitent exorcism of its age-old anti-Semitism, and an appropriation of the passion for social justice of the prophets. Niebuhr, a persistent critic of Roman Catholic cultural and doctrinal rigidity, also expressed a growing appreciation for its insights and new evidences of flexibility especially manifest in the Second Vatican Council. In particular, Niebuhr acknowledged in 1969 a new appreciation for the "intellectual, theological, and moral creativities of the Jesuits."[3]

Niebuhr continued to be a major figure on the Union Seminary faculty (later appointed vice-president as well as professor of social ethics) and engaged in friendly running debates with colleagues John Bennett, Paul Tillich, and Henry Pitney van Dusen. With its potent combination of biblical commitment and social and political action, Christian realism began to make its presence felt in a new breed of church leader: the theologian, pastor,

---

3. Reinhold Niebuhr, "Toward Intra-Christian Endeavors," *The Christian Century*, Vol. LXXXVI, No. 53 (December 31, 1969), 1664.

church executive, missionary, and layperson influenced to one extent or another by Niebuhrian themes. Representative of these various types were Roger L. Shinn, who succeeded Niebuhr at Union in the chair of Applied Christianity (later named the Reinhold Niebuhr chair); George William Webber, founder of the East Harlem Protestant Parish and later president of New York Biblical Seminary; Truman Douglass, leading spirit in the affairs of the National Council of Churches and pioneer for church involvement in human issues; and Martin Luther King Jr., who in a BBC interview shortly before his death described Niebuhr and Gandhi as the major intellectual influences in his life.

In the midst of the joys of a growing family and a lively conjugal partnership, considerably strained, however, by an almost frenetic pace here and abroad, the postwar period brought with it serious evidence of stress. Niebuhr underwent treatment for a critical brain illness and after extended hospitalization, he was forced to curtail activity for many months. While regaining most of the use of his speech and some of his arm movement, he was not able to undertake the globe-trotting and ambitious writing projects of former days. Along with the physical hardships of that time, Niebuhr testified to a spiritual depression. Now known to be a normal outcome of the kind of brain impairment he experienced, the fact that he could not "come out of it" by his own effort exacerbated his disappointment with himself and his prognosis.[4] The reflection generated during this recovery period prompted Niebuhr to search more deeply into the dynamics of selfhood and the significance of the intimate interpersonal as-

4. See "Epilogue: A View of Life from the Sidelines" in Robert McAfee Brown, *The Essential Reinhold Niebuhr* (New Haven: Yale University Press, 1986).

pects of human existence. That rumination is reflected in some of his writings of the period, such as *The Self and the Dramas of History* (1955).

While private commitments clamored for neglected attention, the public was far from forgotten. Association with political molders and shakers continued. His books and periodical commentary showed that his major interests now lay in the field of political encounter, especially international affairs. In *The Children of Light and the Children of Darkness* (1944), *The Structure of Nations and Empires* (1959), and *Faith and Politics* (1968), as well as in *Christianity and Crisis* editorials throughout the same period, Niebuhr's fertile mind was exercised with national and global developments. His *Faith and History* (1949) was a mark of his effort to blend theological and political interests, although in subsequent years the latter came into the foreground.

1960 to 1971: Creative Retirement

Although full relinquishment of responsibilities at Union Seminary came in 1960, it is difficult to draw a neat retirement line in the life of Niebuhr. His services were sought by the Institute for Advanced Studies in Princeton, and he was active in the Center for the Study of Democratic Institutions at Santa Barbara, California. In the years after formal classroom teaching he served as a consultant, if not guru, for countless political and theological inquiries. While in 1966 he left behind him the Riverside Drive apartment for the quieter life of Stockbridge, Massachusetts, friends, visitors, and interviewers continued their pilgrimage to him, and correspondence and writings proceeded at a restricted but nonetheless sprightly pace.

In the 1960s Niebuhr wrote perceptively about issues in both church and world. Long anguished by the "American dilemma" and involved in ministry to it from the days in Detroit, participation in a Mississippi Delta cooperative, and the founding of the Fellowship of Southern Churchmen in the thirties, he was heartened by the civil rights movement of the sixties and gave it his enthusiastic support. On the international scene he was an early opponent, with longtime associate Hans Morgenthau, of the Vietnam War (although not early enough for some of Niebuhr's critics). To Ronald Stone, one of his young interpreters who edited *Faith and Politics* and has subsequently written *Professor Reinhold Niebuhr: A Mentor to the Twentieth Century,* Niebuhr gave some astute observations on the current issues of domestic and international concern.[5] Political commentary continued in such studies as *A Nation So Conceived* (1963) and *Man's Nature and His Communities* (1965).

Niebuhr never lacked opponents. During this period, however, he was getting a new kind of opposition — now nursed on Niebuhrian themes, themselves. From both right and left, they either gave his thought a conservative turn or they actively rebelled against formerly espoused postulates. Thus Will Herberg, Drew University professor of religion who was a close friend and interpreter of an earlier Niebuhr, became numbered among the writers for William Buckley's *National Review,* and Robert Fitch, social ethics faculty member at the Pacific School of Religion, launched diatribes against innovators in theology, morality, and mission. Meanwhile, William Hamilton, a leading exponent of the "death of God" theology, expressed regret over his own earlier captivity to Niebuhrian emphases.

The most sustained and carefully delineated departure from

5. Ronald H. Stone, "An Interview with Reinhold Niebuhr," *Christianity and Crisis,* Vol. XXIX, No. 4 (March 17, 1969), 48-52.

early discipleship in this period was found in political critique and given most forceful interpretation by Richard Shaull. Supporter and interpreter of revolutions in the Third World, Shaull was receptive to the thrust of the New Left (he had served as missionary in Latin America for twelve years), but he believed that the symbols which served Niebuhr so well in illuminating another era of history did not make contact with later decades. He held that Niebuhrian realism, transposed to a new era, settles its adherents too comfortably into the establishment, blunts the edge of radical social criticism, and silences the notes of human possibilities and hopes.[6]

In a limited way, Niebuhr continued the conversation with his critics, taking exception to the "death of God" theology's insensitivity to mystery, grieving at rightist applications of his thoughts, and continuing to affirm the relevance of realism, yet with increasing accent on the possibilities of history, a theme that was always latent in his thoughts. However, it was through the work of such interpreters as John Bennett and Roger Shinn that the dialogue continued with the new theologians of revolution and hope.[7]

Reinhold Niebuhr died peacefully on June 1, 1971, after long and sometimes excruciating periods of debilitation and impairment, periods in which he nevertheless pressed himself to work. At the memorial service in Stockbridge, Massachusetts, Rabbi Abraham Heschel said,

He appeared among us like a sublime figure out of the Hebrew Bible. . . . Niebuhr's life was a song in the form of deeds,

6. Richard Shaull, "Theology and the Transformation of Society," *Theology Today,* Vol. XXV, No. 1 (April 1968), 23-36.

7. John Bennett, Roger L. Shinn, et al., "Christian Realism: A Symposium," *Christianity and Crisis,* Vol. XXVIII, No. 14 (August 5, 1968), 175-90.

a song that will go on for ever. Revered, beloved Reinhold: in the words of the Psalmist,

> You are the fairest of the sons of men,
> Grace is poured upon your lips
> Therefore God has blessed you for ever.[8]

Elements in the Niebuhrian Mode of Life

From this rapid overview of Niebuhr's life, five characteristics stand out as components in the practice of living that ought to make their contribution to later generations.

1. Long before it became stylish to speak of "action research" or the "engagement-reflection methodology," or "praxis" as the context of theology, Reinhold Niebuhr "did" his theology in the setting of the pressing human issues of his day. Christian realism was hammered out in the midst of his participation in the struggles against political, economic, and social tyranny. As there could be in his theology no divorce of God from the world, so act was wedded to thought in Christian faith.

2. Niebuhr engaged culture and took seriously its formative figures. Not only his politics but also his Christian apologetic in sociological, philosophical, and psychological idiom brought him into constant contact with those outside the Christian community, including many alien to any religious organization or profession. He affirmed the good things he saw in them, gave the weight of his own prestige to chastising the church for its failure to approach their level of insight or commitment, and allied himself in their causes for intellectual advance and social

8. Richard Wightman Fox, *Reinhold Niebuhr: A Biography* (New York: Pantheon Books, 1985; paperback, San Francisco: Harper & Row, 1986), 293.

justice. He lost no time, as well, in exploding their illusions and pretensions.

3. Niebuhr's ministry found its center of gravity in the seminary, not the university. Together with his early pastorate, his service to denominational and ecumenical agencies points to a kind of involvement that took seriously the church as well as the world, and acted from within the faith community. A prophet he was to a rebellious people and, like his biblical forebears who had a lover's quarrel with the covenant community, he was a "critic-in-residence."

4. His participation in public institutions was buttressed by a warm and deep personal and interpersonal life. Graced by a sustaining family in his earlier years, Niebuhr sought and found in his adulthood the supportive community of wife and children which embodied the I and Thou themes of Martin Buber, to which he was drawn in his theology. The wide circle of students, former students, and compatriots in church and secular activity represented yet another expression of a pilgrimage which thrived on the communal and contributed to it. And at the profoundest level of the intimate, in introspective analysis and prayer, Niebuhr, like one of his mentors, Augustine, was an explorer of the hidden heights and depths.

5. He was free from captivity to the givens. This freedom is part of what June Bingham in her biography calls "the courage to change."[9] Others describe it as pragmatism. But it is more than openness to correction, more than adaptability. Niebuhrian freedom is the refusal to be caught on the horns of the conventional dilemmas, to be put in the box of predictable alternatives and constructs. He knew that human thought is never quite "right,"

9. June Bingham, *Courage to Change* (New York: Charles Scribner's Sons, 1961; republished 1972; also, Lanham, Md.: University Press of America, 1993).

composed as it is of conclusions drawn at the particular horizons of each viewer. Niebuhr was free enough to move theologically to the right and politically to the left, to defend the paradox when others could only see the orthodox, to discover the maneuvering room between doctrinaire options, and to move in fresh and unforeseen ways beyond rigid polarities. Perhaps this can best be described as a freedom for the future, a quality much coveted in times oriented to the "not yet."

chapter 2

THEOLOGICAL ROOTS

S ome say that Niebuhr was really not a theologian but a political analyst, or at best a moralist. This judgment ignores or diminishes the deep roots of Christian reflection from which Niebuhr's social acumen and action sprang. While not set forth in the conventional categories of the systematician, they account for the rich flowering of "political shoots" to which we shall subsequently turn.

The center of Niebuhr's thought is anthropology, his understanding of humankind before God and where it is headed. The most extended diagnosis of these questions is found in his Gifford Lectures, *The Nature and Destiny of Man,* but it runs as well through all his works and is implicit in every observation made on the passing scene. Characteristically, his teaching emerged in the midst of a struggle with other options, particularly those with political implications and constituencies. We find our way into his thought through that turbulence and the great cultural premises that agitated it.

Twin Errors: Naturalism and Idealism

The anthropological illusions of a secular society are the source of its social disasters. Modern culture is of a divided mind on the question of human nature. Its miscalculations come in two basic varieties: naturalism and idealism.

Naturalism is struck by the affinities between human beings and their natural incubator. We are creatures of our genes, our urges, our sensory input. Such a view comes in many sizes and shapes. It may explain our behavior in terms of body chemistry, hereditary predispositions, psychological forces, racial, sexual, and age factors, climate, geography, economic and social impulses and conditioning, or combinations thereof. The self is seen, at the most, as conscious subject determined by internal and external forces or, at the least, as a simple object in nature's chain of cause and effect. Talk of an "I" free to shape its future is illusory. Naturalism is as skeptical about a unity of human consciousness as it is about a cosmic Self.

Within the presuppositions of naturalism, two modern versions stand out prominently: the empirical and the romantic. The former believes that humankind must learn to live by nature's laws, discerned by the scientific method. The latter, in flight from the corruptions of reason, counsels immersion in the passions and innocencies of nature.

Idealism locates our essence in a transnatural capacity, primarily the quality of reason. Its rationalist perspective is characterized by two assumptions. For one, it draws a sharp line between body and mind. A dualism of this sort denies the organic relation between thought and extension that characterizes naturalism. Secondly, idealism identifies virtue with reason and evil with the passions of nature. To cure human ills, it proposes to activate reason and slough off the inertias of "animality."

Niebuhr traces in considerable detail the lively dynamics within and between these types, noting classic and modern developments, nuances, inconsistencies, interactions, and their social effects. For example, he believes that individuality tends to be destroyed by both naturalism and idealism. The former, in its nineteenth century romantic phase, began by affirming the unique self. But it evolved toward stress upon the individuality of the state, a thesis which prepared the way for the totalitarian brutalities of the twentieth century. Idealism, which discovers dimensions of self unknown to naturalism and therefore knows something of human particularity, finally annihilates individuality in an abstract universalism. It also plays its own role, via Hegel's deification of the state as the historical expression of universal mind, in laying the groundwork for later movements of national self-glorification.

Both anthropologies have a high opinion of human nature and are confident of its future. Either reason or natural vitalities are to be trusted and will soar if the drags and lags can be eliminated. Each point of view finds particular institutions as the embodiment of human defiance of nature or reason's laws. Each draws the conclusion, therefore, that the elimination of priestcraft, tyrannical government, an oppressive class or faulty economic organization, or inept education will solve the human problem.

Both naturalism and idealism assert that the evidence for such an ascent is in the making. An immanent force is at work in history (material or biological according to naturalism, and rational according to idealism) that guarantees upward movement. Society has progressed, and it can and will flow toward its fulfillment.

Niebuhr believed that these conceptions of humanity militate against the facts as they can be perceived by human experience in its widest sense, and thus do not provide an adequate basis for responsible personal and social living. We shall explore in more detail the tools Niebuhr used to discriminate between true and false readings of the human situation. For the time being, we simply note that the options of modern culture prove futile in the long run.

But there is another choice. It is variously described as that of prophetic religion, biblical religion, the Judeo-Christian tradition, the Christian faith, or the Hebraic strain. This alternative illumines human choices and can be validated by our common experience, although commitment to it comes only through the act of penitence and faith and not by argumentation. This option saves us from pretension, complacency, and naivete on the one hand, and despair and flight from the human struggle on the other. We shall attempt to describe it in terms of the dimensions, dynamics, and destiny of humanity.

The Dimensions of Personhood

In contrast to naturalistic and idealistic reductionisms, Niebuhr describes the self in a now-famous phrase as the creature who "lives at the juncture of nature and spirit." Humankind is neither animal nor angel, but a unique amalgam of both. Let us look at the components in their interrelationships.

The Person as Animal

As the naturalists rightly insist, the self is intimately linked to the physio-biological matrix from which it springs. It is "subject to its vicissitudes, compelled by its necessities, driven by its impulses, confined within the brevity of the years which nature permits."[1] We are born of woman and marked by hereditary strain, are as

1. Reinhold Niebuhr, *The Nature and Destiny of Man,* Vol. 1 (New York: Charles Scribner's Sons, 1941), 3; also one-volume edition, 1948, 1953, 1964.

dependent on parent as any animal, must eat, be protected from the elements, urinate, defecate, inhabit space, socialize, procreate, and die. We are subject to conditioning from outside and drives from within. We are, therefore, "lived" by nature.

The Person Is More

But nature is also "lived" by the self. We are conditioned but not programmed. A tiny control tower of spirit thrusts itself above the conditioning factors. From that perch the self looks out on its immersion in natural processes and seeks to bring some coherence and direction to the ebb and flow.

One of the notable dimensions of spirit is reason — the *nous, logos, ratio* that so captured the attention of Greek culture and since has been the distinguishing feature of the human for rationalists. Reason is the capacity to form general concepts. As thinking animals, we employ the instrument of logic to sort out the stimuli that bombard us, to arrange the multifarious pushes and pulls into communicable patterns and ideas. With this power to conceptualize and order the flow of life, the self stands outside, transcends, the natural.

Rationalism identifies an aspect of the self but fails to assess another dimension of spirit. The quintessential "I" ascends the highest steps in the tower of selfhood and there looks back upon the reasoning process itself. Here is a consciousness aware of consciousness, a transcendence that includes not only the capacity to think but to think about oneself in the act of thinking and thus "self-transcendence." An elusive "I" stands out of range of our mightiest efforts to net it. We can never get "in back of" that self which rises above itself in "indefinite regression." Theologians such as Augustine have explored its reaches, laying bare memory and foresight as factors in self-transcendence. Philosophers have remarked upon self-determination as a prominent quality of this central selfhood. Mystics have plunged into the depths of personal self-awareness where few have been able to follow, to report the contours of this difficult terrain. But the ordinary person, by thoughtful introspection, can also discern the reality of an I which in its freedom surveys itself — past, present, and future — and its world, seeks to affect its destiny, and believes it can. Even those who deny the reality of this final dimension of selfhood are forced to presuppose it in their very denial, whenever they use the word "I" and urge others to accept their determinism.

We have described spirit rather abstractly. However, a content and texture are associated with it. The higher reaches of selfhood are pervaded by a sense of being related to and claimed by a source and standard outside the self. This awareness expresses itself in a homelessness of the spirit, an inability to locate any meaning worthy of final trust in the world of nature and history. It is informed also with an inchoate perception that what it does is out of accord with what the self most essentially is called to be. And it is furnished also with a dim instinct of what that mandate is, namely, that life can be fulfilled only in affirmation of, and harmony with, other lives.

So far our analysis has employed the common currency of secular and philosophical language. But we have reached a point where description of the "facts" available to honest introspection moves on to interpretation and hence to the leap of faith. Niebuhr attributes the human sense of being grasped and judged as having its source in the pressure of an Other on the borders of personal awareness. The substance of the mandate which impinges, and the guilt which is generated by the breach of that mandate, is that Other's law of love. The structure through which God makes the divine presence felt in the conscience of a person is the "image of God" in humanity.

Code Language: The Image of God and Our Creatureliness

While Niebuhr includes reason in the image of God, the dialogue in personal subjectivity with another Claimant more closely defines the *imago Dei*. The situation is compared to an eye which has lost its sight but retains its shape and structure. So the self may fail to live out its original purpose of love toward God and humanity (it has lost the "likeness of God"), but it retains enough of the original design to be aware of what it is made for and restive with what it is not (it still has the "image of God"). Thus the image is that capacity of freedom in a person which reflects the freedom of God and is fashioned to fulfill itself in the perfect freedom of self-giving. The freedom is there, dimly aware of its source and end.

Again in contrast to some cultural tendencies, particularly idealist ones, Niebuhr views the self which lives at the confluence of nature and spirit as an unqualified unity. Spirit is not segregated from, or uninfluenced by, the body as it is in classic and contemporary rationalism. The mind is the body's mind, as in Hebrew thought the soul is the blood's breath. While psychosomatic evidence documents this conviction, it is the biblical belief to which this affirmation is finally traced. Pointing also to this unity is the doctrine of the resurrection of the body, to be distinguished from the Greek notion of immortality which viewed the soul as detachable at death from the unworthy body. Another biblical thesis about the unity of the self is the doctrine of God as Creator. The God of biblical faith is no divine Mind who orders a neutral or recalcitrant materiality. Rather, God is both vitality and form, the Author of heaven and earth, things spiritual and material, and manifesting this commonality in the creation of a whole person.

As a human being is made in the togetherness of body and spirit, so the person is designed for unity within the human family. We have spoken of the fundamental dependence of the individual on others for physical survival and growth. Humankind is fulfilled in spirit as well as nature in and through its communal relationships. At the most basic level, our symbol life, our language, is made possible through community. In the higher reaches of the human spirit, the self is so designed that it cannot be fulfilled unless it lives in harmony with other selves. That oneness itself is not achievable unless persons give themselves for their neighbor. Thus the ground of human life is sociality, and its law is love.

The Dynamics of Personhood

Anxiety

Life at the juncture just described is not an easy one. Niebuhr finds its most poignant ambiguity in the ultimate yearnings fostered by the image yet frustrated by creaturely moorings. Developing an existentialist motif, shaped particularly by Kierkegaard's analysis of the human predicament, he speaks of an appetite for the infinite whetted by a spirit that is in touch with the transtemporal and made for a goal outside of itself. The spirit, which rises above its natural rootages to view a greater possibility, discovers that its expectations stand under the threat of finitude. Human beings thirst for the security of the absolute, but death seems to render that hope spurious. A pilot trained to fly is mysteriously grounded. The enigma of hobbled flight sets up in us a profound anxiety. We must secure our ego somehow and prove that our lives are not in vain.

Anxiety is the precondition of sin. It does not force sin into being, for ideally anxiety could be allayed by a serenity derived from a more ultimate security than history can furnish. In fact, anxiety could be transmuted into new levels of creativity. As it works out, anxiety proves to be our undoing: the snake in the Genesis myth beguiles Adam and Eve (an account to be taken "seriously, although not literally"), a story that describes the universal tendency of anxious persons to look out for number one.

Idolatry

When we choose ourselves as the objects of first loyalty, we displace the One who rightly deserves that allegiance. Our primal sin, therefore, is idolatry, the will to be God. It bends the urge planted in us to give ourselves in absolute devotion back toward the self alone and its programs. The action is described in Genesis (3:5) as the wish of an incurved self to usurp the prerogatives of Deity, to "be like God." Here is "unbelief," therefore, a primordial self-alienating "self-love" or "pride" that is the lethal constant in human life.

This "self-regarding impulse" lies at the very center of human personality, in the will. Naturalism locates the trouble in human reason and therefore assumes that a plunge into or alignment with natural vitalities will cure the ailment. Idealism holds that evil lies in either a passion or an ignorance that can be corrected by larger doses of reason. Niebuhr, on the other hand, finds the human sickness to be in the very freedom which rises above both nature and reason. Since the self is corrupted at its very core, naturalistic and idealistic solutions are an exercise in futility. Human perversity will assert itself in every new configuration arranged by their optimistic proposals, as it is a stubborn parasite on human freedom. The enlargement of the very capacity that is singular to humans therefore carries with it the threat of destruction as well as the promise of creativity.

Human egoism displays a particular intransigence at the level of social institutions. Collectivities such as nations and economic systems are especially prone to a destructive self-interest, magnifying the sin that is in the heart of the individual. While Niebuhr summed up this thesis in the title of his early work, *Moral Man and Immoral Society,* in later years he said it should more properly have read, "immoral man and even more immoral society."

Privateering

Self-elevation, "playing God," takes shapes commensurate with the dimensions of human nature. Sin can express itself in a will to dominate, to lord it over others. Our will to power is related to our unique stature as spirit providing us with the occasion to think of ourselves more highly than we ought to think. Privateering is pride in a second and derivative sense, the imperialism which forces others to bow the knee before one's own claims and agendas. An understanding of Niebuhr's view of sin as pride requires the grasp of this important distinction.

Flight

Self-elevation can express itself also as a will to powerlessness, as retreat from responsibility into finitude's cavernous escape routes. Borrowing and refining the Augustinian category of concupiscence (not confining it to the notion that it is transmitted by coitus nor limited to "fleshly" sins), Niebuhr speaks of it as a sensuality which seeks to cope with anxiety by flight into forgetfulness and ultimately into self-forgetfulness. It includes the escape into animality, bourgeois mediocrity, and the rat race on the one hand, and lassitude or apathy on the other.

The Smokescreen: Self-righteousness

Our idolatrous self-regarding impulses, interlaced as they are with freedom, regularly hide themselves behind the mask of self-righteousness. Sin is not a simple self-deification but one that cloaks itself in virtue. Niebuhr shows the similarity between biblical realism about human "pharisaism" and the concept of ideology in Marx (regnant ideas in class society as tools of the ruling class) and rationalization in Freud (giving good reasons for real reasons). Each exposes the feverish human effort to veil our self-centeredness in the garments of the wise and the good. The biblical eye sees more deeply than secular realisms, for the latter do not indict themselves for the same pretensions they see in others.

Human Destiny

Ranged against our self-regarding impulses are forces which struggle to contain and redeem them. God confronts them in a history destined for another end.

Counterforce 1: Judgment in History and the Self

In arrogance we may defy the law of love, but we cannot defy it absolutely. As the law of life, anything less than mutuality is self-destructive. This lesson is driven home vividly in the conduct of nations and their leaders, as the prophets took pains to point out. Blatant imperialism brings in its wake historical punishment. God acts through this law of mutuality to bring the mighty from their seats. As the essential pattern of life is unity, its violators will pay the price when they tear its fabric. In fact, the consequence of this confrontation is the "wrath of God." Niebuhr sometimes describes this recoil of life's essential structure as a "rough justice," for it cannot be detailed with philosophical nicety. Periods come in which the imperious do prosper for there is no neat punishment commensurate with crime. Yet over the long haul, the law cannot be breached without disastrous effects.

The counterpart to a large-scale judgment is the outworking of justice in the inner recesses of selfhood. Inasmuch as the self still carries the marks of its essential mandate to live for others, its self-preoccupation is shadowed by guilt. A nagging uneasiness with anything less than self-giving cannot be erased as long as human freedom itself is not aborted. This uneasiness is the fruit of the constant divine impingement on the spirit dimension of selfhood.

Counterforce 2: Healing in History and the Self

In earlier years, and again in much later ones, Niebuhr spoke warmly of a "common grace" turned loose in the world. The arena in which it does its work, such as in the family and in face-to-face relationships, tends to be on a much smaller scale than that in which judgment manifests itself. However, it is not altogether absent from the dealings of nations. While the latter prove more fertile soil for chastisement appropriate to the collective evils to which humans are so prone, Providence works through the residual moral sense of political entities, a fact that may startle and disprove a too-consistent cynicism about the affairs of nations. This modicum of responsibility may express itself in care for a nation suffering starvation or a sober restraint on the temptation to exploit another's weakness. It is also manifest in the rich elaboration of human potentiality that appears in history, and the cultural and scientific fecundity that moves society. A latter-day appreciation of the Renaissance moved Niebuhr to note these workings, formerly muted.

Common grace is more often noted in the intimacies of life. Parental care can provide a sense of security which frees the growing self in turn to love others. Niebuhr notes as well a conjugal love that both ministers in disaster and liberates the partners to larger meanings. Also, in the forgiveness and compassion of friends and associates, he saw a "reflection and refraction" of a more ultimate Mercy. And in the nourishment of the spirit by the past's heritage, and of the body by the intricate network of natural and social relationships, he discovered as well the action of a benevolent God.

While Niebuhr had relatively little to say about the world of nature, and often what was said stressed its brutality if not its malevolence, allusions may be found, particularly in his earlier writings, to grace at work in nature. He notes that a benevolent natural alchemy, if not overtaxed by personal greed and/or stupid uses of science technology, will save an urban mass from destruction by its own pollutants. This kind of healing, which can be seen in marvels that run from the body's restorative powers to the recuperation of a tree struck by lightning, is often ignored or missed by a society of cities. Nevertheless it is retained by those who live close to the soil and should be honored by the religious imagination as a sign of a larger good at work.

A Special Work of Hope

An important clue to Niebuhr's understanding of what decisive action God takes to overcome human rebellion, and who in fact God is, is found in the use of the analogy of personal relationship. A human being may survey the external shape and behavior of another and grasp something about the nature and character of that second self. But the depth of the other's being is not exposed until the one that is viewed as an object becomes a subject, uncovering the self's inner thoughts and shedding light on the meaning of overt actions. When the other speaks the disclosing word, the first person is drawn into a new relationship, out of the role of dispassionate spectator and into that of personal communion.

The processes of historical judgment and grace described above are similar to the external actions of another person. We experience them, and can even grasp something of their meaning. Thus God's overt work is a "general revelation." But the deeper significance of what they confront and dimly perceive is lost upon them until the Self chooses to reveal the inner depths of his heart and mind, a "special revelation."

In an obscure slice of Hebrew history the divine Self-disclosure begins. Prophets declare that God has a bone to pick not only with the impious nation but also with the people of the Covenant. History is not simply a contest between the just and the unjust but a struggle in which even the righteous set themselves against the Lord. Within the messianic tradition in Judaism, the prophet looks for the day when a just and merciful God will extirpate evil and reclaim the lost, establishing the Kingdom. But it is never clear how the justice of this God which brooks no evil can be satisfied, and mercy prevail.

The enigma of justice and mercy is resolved in the final disclosure of who God is, in Jesus Christ. The life, teaching, and death of Jesus embody the perfect law of love. The pattern of self-giving clarifies the Source of the unity by which the world lives. Jesus' uncalculating love demonstrates the paradox of a self-offering which must animate mutuality if that latter harmony is not to be corrupted by a prudence still caught in the circle of self-interest. But it also dramatizes the fate of heedless care on worldly turf. Perfect Love plus sin equals crucifixion.

The cross and its sequel, the resurrection, are transactions that illumine the unsolved problem of the Old Testament and release a power that can cope with the self's own sin. Golgotha reveals a Love that absorbs the punishment which an unsentimental Justice requires. The God who suffers brings together justice and mercy. In the cross we see a sacrificial love that takes up into itself the punishment which justice demands. The resurrection announces that this self-offering does not end in futility. The happening on a hill corresponds to the deepest level of the structures of reality and its ultimate issue. The Pauline construal of the Galilean story corresponds to Jesus' own understanding of the message of the Kingdom of God. He viewed himself as herald and first fruit of the inbreaking waves of a New Commonwealth of peace and righteousness and pointed ahead to its fulfillment at the end of history.

To return to our analogy of personal relationship, God showed "what was on the divine mind" in the central events of Jesus. A long-suffering Love bears history forward, one whose Word and Act shouldered the consequences of human rebellion and thereby assured the fulfillment of the divine intention. And as in the human relation, in which loving self-disclosure draws the other into communion, so in this self-offering, those who have the eyes to see and the ears to hear are driven to penitence and faith. To penitence, because they discover their own implication in humankind's wounding of God and through penitence, faith. In genuine repentance the self is broken and authentic shattering continues as a lifelong vocation. Faith is born as the self's trust that its guilt is conquered by a suffering Love.

To faith is added hope. The rich and murky symbols of the Apocalypse display the promise that the incompleteness and ambiguities of self and society will be overcome at "the end of history." The Christian doctrine of the End conceives the fulfillment of the biblical hope as a transfiguration different from anything possible "in history." It thus avoids the illusions of those who claim too much for their own achievements or plans. As the vision is "out ahead," and thus in some relationship with our own life on earth, it also calls into question notions of fulfillment which dismiss the significance of this life and work for an escape into an eternity "above history." The symbol of Last Things, without literal portrayal of "the furniture of heaven and the temperature of hell," affirms the continuity with, and importance of, the historical pilgrimage and our efforts in it. It also dignifies our individuality and assures the solidity of its rootage in a final reality which is not identifiable with our manageable and conventional visibilities.

To hope is added love. And for one remembered by many as among the world's most searching moralists, we devote a full section to this third theological virtue.

The Works of Love

The Test: Social Revelance

The issue of faith and hope is love. The works of love, their meaning and application, formed the center of gravity of Niebuhr's thought. Early in his Detroit pastorate he remarked that the ministry was taking on a new luster as he gave more attention to its ethical concerns and less to its metaphysical quandaries. The light shed by Christian faith on the issues of war and peace, international relations, poverty, economic justice, race, and sex continued to be focal throughout his life. So the Niebuhrian refrain, "By their fruits you shall know them."

Concern for social implications and applications can be described as a moral pragmatism. He evaluated concepts, secular or churchly, according to their capacity to illumine or provide incentive for the solution of human problems. A favorite two-pronged test was the ability of an idea to avoid the "Scylla" of fanaticism or the "Charybdis" of despair. The former, a distortion of human freedom, represents the self-righteous fury which sooner or later brings chaos to persons and nations. The latter, a perversion of human ties to nature, often the result of a shattered megalomania, is a flight from moral responsibility. Variations on these two poles include sentimentality, self-righteousness, and complacency on the one hand, and mediocrity, lassitude, and sensuality on the other. Thus the question of how best to execute the ethical test became the forum in which an "apologetic" dialogue was carried out.

While the moral test can invalidate an idea that could not produce fruits, and lend credence to ones that could, it was not offered simplistically as the method of final accreditation of the truth of the Christian faith. A good moral record assures a thesis of candidacy. But Christian faith, as a personal commitment, cannot be generated by moral argument. Genuine conviction is a penitence and faith born of the Holy Spirit.

Perfectionism and Its Problems

Niebuhr's earliest wrestling with the major questions of a love ethic came in his struggle with pacifism. Religious pacifists read the rigorous New Testament admonitions to turn the cheek and go the second mile as literal counsels of nonviolence in personal conduct and public affairs. A frequent corollary was the assumption that this behavior meshed with the deepest structures of human life. Self-abnegation would be reciprocated in kind, and social problems would find their solution by obedience to the radical selflessness set forth in the Sermon on the Mount. An essential goodness in each person, a spark of divinity, would be fanned into a blaze of goodwill by the action of those who practice the ethics of sacrificial love.

Niebuhr honored the pacifist testimony to selflessness. It is the pinnacle of the Christian ethic as embodied in the life of Christ manifesting the suffering love of God. Anything less than self-giving does indeed inject poison into the world's bloodstream. Further, Niebuhr believed that the small enclaves of pacifist witness, particularly those with religious roots such as the Mennonites, serve as the reminder of the heights of Christian expectation and as a judgment of conscience on human violence and self-aggrandizement.

One ingredient, however, is missing in the pacifist calculus: human sin. The absence of that factor skews the pacifists' analysis of behavior and accounts for the futility of their program of social change. Human self-regarding impulses make their impact felt in several ways. For one, recognition of their stubborn persistence in those to be won by our nonviolence is missing. Given universal sin, the enemy is prone to interpret the gesture of nonviolence as weakness, rather than to be humbled by its kindnesses. The result is not only the crucifixion of the nonviolent, which an authentic pacifist is fully ready to accept, but also the sacrifice of those innocents and values which might otherwise be protected, if less pacific means had been resorted to. The magnifying of the exploitative instinct in large collectivities renders the pacifist counsel even more dangerous as a political guideline. The Nazi phenomenon was a dramatic case in point. Not only the annihilation of the Jew but the crumbling of the Western charter of freedom and justice would have resulted from the totalitarian juggernaut, if the way of nonviolence had been chosen.

The rejection of an ideological pacifism does not preclude, however, a pragmatic one. Niebuhr believed that in dealing with the relatively civilized British conscience, a Gandhi could effect change by passive resistance. And in the 1960s Niebuhr acknowledged the effectiveness of Martin Luther King Jr.'s tactics in a conscience-stricken America, exposed as well to world opinion. However, he consistently underscored the naivete of a doctrinaire pacifism which based its strategies on the fundamental goodness of humanity, ignoring the tragic consequences of its proposed actions.

Niebuhr saw yet another illusion of pacifism to be the failure to probe its own motives and conduct. He sometimes wondered out loud about the bitterness of the attack of pacifists on those who took issue with their position. The impossibility of the ideal was demonstrated by the very ones who so loudly espoused it.

The Relevance of an Impossible Ideal

If the absolute love ethic could not be applied directly to human affairs, then what use was it? Niebuhr cited at least five ways in which it was relevant as an "impossible possibility" (a term later abandoned because it lent itself too easily to misunderstanding), some of which we have already alluded to in Niebuhr's affirmation of the pacifist's role:

- Absolute love is testimony to the fundamental structure of the universe. To save one's life is to lose it. Self-concern has in it the seeds of destruction.
- The love absolute represents a lure toward higher approximations of neighborly concern and a judge upon lower ones. We cannot rest easily in any setting less than that of self-giving harmony of life with life.
- Unstinting *agape* witnesses to the paradox that the spirit of selflessness is the only condition upon which mutuality itself can thrive. The give-and-take that harmony requires cannot be launched or sustained by prudence, for that kind of calculation

is itself caught in the trap of self-interest and will tend to poison human relationships.

- Because there are residual traces of grace and goodness in human self and society, there are some points of contact for self-giving love. This is particularly true of the more intimate human relationships. It can trigger response in kind. Sacrificial care can move others to penitence and reciprocating kindness. Thus there are some tangents in history to what is, in the last analysis, a transhistorical standard.

- Perfect sacrificial love, eminently displayed in the life and death of Jesus, is the only rock on which the obtuseness of humanity can finally be shattered. Here the dim perception that the self is made for selflessness is clarified. Before the cross the penitence is born that calls into question the imperious self, and faith in the divine forgiveness is nourished.

Reachable Norms

While a love absolutism serves these purposes, it cannot provide viable guidelines for day-to-day ethics, especially social ethics. For this we must express love in derivative norms that presuppose the insights of original sin/universal self-regard, translating absolute love into realizable goals.

Mutual love is such a first derivative norm. Kindred to sacrificial love, it wills the harmony of life with life. But the former has an element of prudence in contrast to the latter's uncalculating spontaneity and self-giving. In mutual love, the self affirms the interest of other selves with an eye on a society which promises self-fulfillment. The limits of this ethic were cited earlier. Also, mutuality is a goal that can be moved toward only at the pace of manifest self-interest. In any case it does serve as a social directive that comes within the range of historical possibility.

A notch below the level of mutual love is equal justice. Reflecting the New Testament absolute, it echoes the "as thyself" of the love injunction. By this standard we are advised to give to each person as much as we claim for ourselves. Justice of any kind presupposes the conflict of life with life and seeks to sort out conflicting claims. Persons deserve their due. In the case of equal justice, equity is that due.

chapter 3

POLITICAL SHOOTS

The title of Niebuhr's book *Faith and Politics* (1968) points to the rhythm we are tracing. His theology and ethics flow naturally toward political reflection and action of two kinds: confrontation with epochal cultural currents and shrewd commentary on, and participation in, the events of the day.

Measuring History's Movements

The major political options of the twentieth century pass in review, as do their premises about human nature and destiny. Let us sample a few of the analyses.

Marxism

Niebuhr moved from an appreciative yet critical opinion of Marxism (in the Depression he accepted the label of "Christian Marxist") to a view in which his disagreements and hostility far outweighed the things that he could acknowledge as corrective of capitalist injustices. We can, however, identify recurring motifs, with emphases that both grow and recede.

The capitalism that threw off the yoke of medieval aristocracy knew about the corruptibility of political power. But freedom from the feudal lord did not produce a just society. The invisible hand of Adam Smith and the presumed laws of the free market that were to produce human welfare did not materialize. Instead, the new bourgeoisie amassed an economic power that caused untold harm. Marx, moved by a passionate humanism, surveyed the effects of nineteenth-century laissez-faire capitalism that brought dehumanization and death to countless workers, and labeled private property as the virus in the system. Niebuhr believed that Marx was correct in pinpointing the economic failures as a source of the era's miseries (although wrong in failing to probe below the profit motive to a more basic level of culpability). Control of human life by an economic elite and its machinery had to be challenged and checked. Until 1948 the solution, for Niebuhr and his associates in the Fellowship of Christian Socialists, lay in the common ownership of the natural resources and the basic means of production. It became increasingly clear, however, that the Marxist program of extirpating evil by removing private property produced a new concentration of power with its attendant corruptibility. Marxist society, blinded by its anthropological illusions, established a new oligarchy with its own tyrannies. Similar naivete plagued democratic socialism, resulting in its failure to provide for incentives and for protection against the exploitation of a persisting self-interest.

Niebuhr moved to a less doctrinaire posture in dealing with the abuses of economic power. The Christian Marxist of the thirties became the Christian pragmatist of the fifties. Property itself, always bearing in it the seeds of injustice when growing inordinately, was seen in a limited way as a method of securing society against the development of political, social, or other economic monoliths. The new pragmatism meant, most of all, that no ideology could be a reliable guide for solving the complex problems of a technological society. Each situation had to be judged on its own merits, with an eye always kept open for the corrupting tendencies of ascending power. Efforts had to be exerted to build balancing structures in the social fabric.

Niebuhr credited Marxism with a deeper perception of human egoism than most secular worldviews. It saw, for instance in its "catastrophism," that those who control society could not be persuaded out of their bastions by reason or preachment. And in its concept of ideology, Marxism exposed the taint of self-interest in professedly objective structures of law, politics, morality, and religion. Because it located the reason for these tendencies in private ownership, it failed to allow for the persistence of self-interest in its own programs and dreams. Thus Marxism fell prey to the mystical glorification of classless society which the facts did not warrant. And it succumbed to a utopianism that either clung fanatically to its delusions, on the one hand, or was driven to despair by the shattering of its dreams, on the other. The era of Stalinist and Russian imperialism was the fruit of utopian fanaticism, and the ex-Marxist dropouts from the social struggle were the children of disillusionment.

While Niebuhr's assessment of Marxism was couched in economic and political terms, he sought to push below these to its fundamental premises about humanity and its destiny. In fact, he sought to show that both Marxism's strengths and weaknesses are traceable more directly to its being a "religion" than an alleged scientific account of social processes. Its passion for justice and dream of a world in which each gives unselfishly and has needs satisfied by society is linked to the Judeo-Christian tradition. Interlaced with this prophetic note is an interpretation of history which locates its origin in a paradisical primitive communism from which humanity fell away by the seductions of private property. But the gods of history will not rest easy with this fall, so the story goes. A mysterious dialectical providence moves by the motors of economic need through succeeding societies to a final denouement in which class polarities come to a head in the Armageddon struggle of late capitalism. At this time, those born to redeem history, the proletariat, are raised up to deliver the final blow to the dragon in a violent paroxysm, whose issue will be a world at one with itself. So reads the creed in the Manifesto that Engels described originally as a "catechism."

Liberalism

As Niebuhr could find in fundamental Marxism no solutions for the twentieth century, he also rejected "liberalism," the other political and social creed that claimed the allegiance of countless contemporaries, particularly his own country's intellectual leadership.

Taking its rise in Renaissance and Enlightenment understandings of humanity, liberal social philosophy believed in the essential goodness of human nature. Trusting especially in human reasonableness, it saw no recalcitrance which could not be eliminated. Yes, progress was impeded by continued ignorance, by passions still clinging from the residues of our animal nature, and by outworn social institutions, but education and moral suasion could overcome these obstacles.

In fact, social scientists were going about their business attempting just that. The obsolete social forms and irrationalities of the past were thought to be progressively eliminated in an inevitable ascent of humanity. History was a satisfying pilgrimage. It showed clear signs of advance and held out the promise of an upward escalator trip. The evolution manifest in nature was also at work on the human plane, moving the race into successively greater degrees of goodwill and harmony.

These sanguine assumptions and expectancies were characteristic of all exponents of the liberal creed, including the pragmatist in the John Dewey tradition and the Social Gospel reformer. Their premises were joined to several other ideas which marked the mainstream movement as bourgeois (although they did not characterize the left end of the spectrum such as the socialist fringe). One was an individualism which held that human dignity is best upheld by freedom from the restraints of the community. Indeed, the human choice to work is out of self-interest, but its results are shaped by benevolent natural processes — crafted by an Invisible Hand — so that the egoism of each eventuates in the well-being of all. Individualism was bourgeois in the way it furnished the rising middle classes with a battle cry against feudal restraints that slowed the engines of commercial and industrial development.

With its suspicion of the communal motif, the individualist spirit of bourgeois liberalism had little time for talk about the social matrix of selfhood. Self-made persons pulled themselves up by their own bootstraps. Those who fell by the wayside were moral dropouts, to be scorned — or, at best, pitied. Society and its structures neither broke them nor saved them. Individuals by the rugged strength of their will and hard work had to make their own way.

Niebuhr characteristically sketched in broad brush strokes the qualities of the liberal creed and then, in equally sweeping but penetrating judgments, lined out an indictment. Liberalism, especially its bourgeois mainstream, was refuted by history itself. It was unprepared for the horrendous sequel to its ascendency. Thus the harmless self-interest it assumed would do its benevolent work turned into a holocaust of starvation, exploitation, and depression for countless millions. And on the heels of that came total government, total wars and programs of genocide which sent reeling the sanguine forecasts of a culture which had assumed that barbarity had been long left behind with the passing of primitive cultures. The contours of its own institutions began to show through the tattered garments of modern society, demonstrating that human beings are much more creatures of their social environment than individualism assumed, making and breaking them by its machinery.

Historical evidence demonstrates, affirmed Niebuhr, that faith in human goodness and reason is misplaced. The human problem is more than cultural lag or lack of social intelligence. The trouble lies at the very center of our being, in a corrupt will. Therefore, every advance in history in which human ingenuity spawns technological growth or social reorganization is not an unambiguous step forward. Along with creativity, which the liberal spirit did unshackle and discern to be limitless, goes the risk of continued and even more devastating forms of destruction. History supplies no evidence that good triumphs over evil.

The miscalculations of individualism must also be corrected by a more organic understanding of human nature. We are not isolated atoms of pure will. We are creatures of nature and social networks which support and can also destroy them.

As with Marxism, so with liberalism; Niebuhr found strengths as well as weakness. While rejecting its unwarranted optimism, he denied as well notions of total depravity and complete cynicism about our society's future. Thus he affirmed in a modest and qualified way the human possibilities which liberalism celebrated, albeit too noisily and uncritically. Openness to the future, readiness to call into question the intellectual or institutional status quo, pursuit of free inquiry, open debate in the marketplace of ideas — all these characteristics of the liberal spirit he believed to be commitments whose loss would be perilous to society.

Key Elements in Critique and Construction

Reality

The error common to both Marxism and liberalism is the failure to detect the depth and persistence of our self-regarding impulses, especially as they mold collectivities. An alternate perspective will have at its center a realistic estimate of human nature, its perversities and the inclination to obscure them. Realism will be alert to any accumulation of power, wary of its temptations, suspicious of its protestations of interest in the common welfare, and committed to the dispersing and democratizing of power, surrounding it with checks and balances.

Because of the disruptive inclinations of human sin, realism will also struggle for that measure of social order which makes human association livable. While checking and equilibrating power is a necessary step toward tolerable justice, this effort assumes a fabric of human community made possible only by the political restraint of egoism, hence the necessity for "order" as a social goal. But realism will also point to that kind of order in which the structures of governance are imposed by the citizenry itself. Liberty is the protection of the people against the tyranny of political power. It is also the context in which the full resources of the community can be uncovered and harnessed for the public weal.

Thus, realism points to the principles of equal power: just distribution of society's resources and opportunities, order that guarantees the social fabric will not be torn by conflicting interests, and freedom to control that order and release its human possibilities.

Vision

While Niebuhr stressed the realistic factors because of the high visibility of over-optimistic estimates of people and their social designs, another political lodestar is also at work. The pull of vision is integral to Niebuhr's political philosophy, as well as the push of reality. While the law of love in its perfectionist form cannot be exported neatly from heaven to earth, it does its work from "out ahead," illumining the path to be traversed, and luring us toward a fuller approximation of its harmonies. Love declares for the dignity of each human being and pleads for the designing of a society in which each life is fulfilled. Christian love, tutored in the sinfulness of the terrain on which it must operate, strives for equal justice, taking its cue from the "as thyself" in the neighbor/love mandate. Another "due," which reflects the dignity accorded each self by love and honors the unique capacity of transcendence associated with that dignity, is political freedom. Some mechanism to insure the implementation of justice and freedom derived from love is needed, as well. Thus the function of government is not only the negative restraint of evil but also the positive guarantee of the fruits of the society to all its participants.

Both reality and vision provide the makings of Niebuhr's political philosophy, the former much more explicitly than the latter, thus warranting the description of Niebuhr's position as "Christian realism." But it should be noted that both from "below" and "above," that is, from the past experience of human recalcitrance and from the future Goal of the human pilgrimage, is to be heard the call for justice, equality, freedom, and order. Fundamental premises about human flourishing and derivative moral mandates are at work in his more general reflections on domestic and international affairs. We turn next to them.

The Nation

The focus on the mature thought of Niebuhr takes us from a variety of Christian socialism to Christian pragmatism. While guided by the postulates cited above, no attempt is made to create a blueprint for the social order. Niebuhr's method is inductive. He begins with the situation and tests it for adequacy, rather than imposing a deductive scheme upon it. He views the political scene in experimental terms, hoping to learn from the mistakes of a venture launched, accommodating to new realities, spurred by new insights. This British "muddling through" approach is related to his conviction that while history is not simply an organism, neither is it an artifact easily contrived by human ingenuity. We work with the givens, molding them experimentally in the double light of reality and vision.

The Struggle for Justice

Niebuhr's analysis and proposals begin with the givens of the liberal West in which he finds himself. Thus, he turns his attention to the struggles in the nineteenth century with dehumanizing industrial baronies. This arrogance of economic power produced the countervailing force of the labor movement. The trade unions demonstrated that the assumptions of a self-regulating capitalism were fictitious. Workers had to organize to protect themselves against the exploitative tendencies of a laissez-faire economy and its power wielders. Moreover, their fight for basic social security required the assistance of government. Accordingly, political power became a weapon in the struggle to check economic power and redress its wrongs. While an earlier and ideological Niebuhr scorned the New Deal as a palliative, he later came to view the Roosevelt era as a laboratory in which many of the inequalities of early capitalism were corrected by a social-welfare pragmatism.

On the heels of the workers' struggle came the human rights fight of African American citizens. Long grieved by the "American dilemma" of a high charter of freedom and equality yet a flagrant abuse of it in the treatment of African Americans, Niebuhr thought the freedom movement, particularly under the leadership of Martin Luther King Jr., would make wise use of social and political power to redress old grievances and give a new sense of dignity to the oppressed. As in the case of blue collar workers, so also with black citizens; not only was elementary justice at stake, but the freedom movement was releasing long-untapped resources among black citizens that would ultimately benefit the whole community.

While government served as a balance wheel to other centers of tempted power and as an instrument of distributive justice, it was itself a power that had to be watched and moderated both from within and without. From within, the wisdom of the country's founders had provided a system of checks and balances — legislative, judicial, and executive. From without, the pluralism of the institutions and interests of a democratic society helped to restrain monolithic tendencies, as did the election system itself.

The Welfare State

Niebuhr saw biblical and Renaissance values combine with the exigencies and dynamics of a technopolitan society to follow a tortuous route of trial and error until it produced the modern "welfare state." He did not believe this vast social experiment was neatly exportable to other societies at different stages of growth, nor did he claim universal validity for it. But for the conditions of a highly developed technological West it seemed to provide a tolerable mix of the best elements of the two competing creeds — planning and freedom — which in their extreme Marxist and bourgeois liberal form had proved inadequate. This mix, which guaranteed maneuvering room for its citizens within an order that acknowledged its responsibility to provide for the basic needs of all (although yet unable to match promise with performance, especially for the poor and for African Americans), succeeded by its cultivation of a variety of centers of power and by a charter with commitments to the well-being of all. Its modest realism about the ways of securing justice, and its modest idealism about the possibilities of achieving it, reflected the human condition itself. That estate suggested the viability of this kind of social arrangement. As Niebuhr put it in one of his memorable epigrams: "Man's capacity for justice makes democracy possible; but man's inclination to injustice makes democracy necessary."[1]

International Affairs

As Marxism and bourgeous liberalism, planning and freedom, provided the foci for Niebuhr's political thought in other areas, so in the sphere of world affairs the giant embodiments of these polarities, the Soviet Union and the United States, occupied the center of his reflection. This is especially true in the years in which Niebuhr exercised a significant influence among political scientists and government leaders. Both Russia and America lived by social myths. Under the battlements of each huddled numerous client nations, as the medieval castle hovered protectively over its constituent lands and towns.

1. Reinhold Niebuhr, *The Children of Light and the Children of Darkness* (New York: Charles Scribner's Sons, 1944), xiii (republished New York: The Macmillan Company, 1979).

Russia

Marxism made its first significant conquest in Russia. While rejected in the European technical society for which it was ideologically designed, it took root in a pastoral culture whose postwar deterioration made it ripe for the ardent revolutionary schemes of Lenin. Using formulas whose reference points were the decadence of late capitalism, Russian communism hauled a peasant society doggedly into a twentieth-century technological setting with a totalitarian grip. The price of that pull was the horrendous brutality of the Stalinist era and the elimination of the harmful step of political democracy which Europe and the West had found to be the prerequisite of a just society. While the Soviet Union successfully negotiated its way into an advanced technology, one which boasted some stunning victories over the less tightly run Western democracies, its life was now in the hands of a political elite vulnerable to the same temptations of power to which the rejected economic oligarchs had fallen prey. As Marxism mistakenly located evil in property as such, it failed to build into its system protection against the corruption to which any structure of power is vulnerable.

The aggrandizing impulse meshed with national self-esteem to generate an imperialism which hid itself under a righteous ideology. Purporting to be the evangelist of a communism out to save the world from bourgeois mendacity, the Soviet Union extended the borders of its influence wherever capitalistic expansion displayed its Achilles' heel or a moribund colonialism beat an undignified retreat. And if any of those gathered under its wing stepped out of line, a Hungary or a Czechoslovakia, that would be too bad. What was originally a more pugnacious imperialism, however, mellowed somewhat as Russia's economy provided more creature comforts to its citizens. Now the old Marxist cry that the proletariat had nothing to lose but its chains sounded a little hollow. Also, the terror of a nuclear war had its sobering effect on the Kremlin. Expansionist propensities took more the turn of aid to developing nations, very similar to the technical assistance of the West, along with support of a more military nature. And here and there agreements were reached to moderate a too calamitous confrontation with the West

As Russia flirted with coexistence, Niebuhr saw a new China rising to claim the title of champion of the world proletariat, declaring Russia a revisionist heretic. Much further from the security reached by the Soviet Union, it was far less ready for accommodation with the West and more explosive in its rhetoric. Also as a nation of color in the way Russia was not, it laid claim to the title of chief antagonist of the wealthy white oppressor. As with Russia, so with China; the ideology, heightened even further by claims to righteous purity, served to hide national ambitions that were beginning to manifest themselves around its borders and beyond.

The United States

Against the Bear and the Tiger, the Eagle saw itself as the protector of herds of weaker game. America, cradled in liberty, driven by a Wilsonian vision of universal self-determination, would protect the old stag and the young fawn from the terrors of the forest. Niebuhr believed that there was enough truth in this myth to include as a plank in U.S. foreign policy the readiness to place limits on the expansionist zeal of Communist nations, especially Russia, which had the technical ability to implement its rhetoric. Of particular importance was the guarding of the European laboratory of social democracy.

American idealism was compounded with its own brand of imperial ambition. Such was manifest in the too-eager desire to impose its democratic traditions, developed in an unusually hospitable environment, on nascent countries not similarly equipped and under a more rapid technological survival time schedule. It was seen as well in a neocolonial economic expansionism in developing countries. Add to this a major miscalculation and some accidents of history, and the result was the anguish of Vietnam. Drawn into a civil war by our ideology of self-determination and the need for naval bases in Asia, America's military prestige became tarnished by the tenacity of effective guerrilla forces. Meanwhile its moral prestige was also soiled by a heavy-handed employment of the new technology of devastation and its reliance upon a suspect military coterie. In our persistence in the war, Niebuhr believed we were encouraging the move we most fear, the enemy's drawing closer to China and to the orthodox Marxism our policy of this period alleged to contain.

While America had arrived at a workable welfare-state democracy for its own technologically advanced society, Niebuhr believed that it should not impose this formula in contests which did not have similar conditions. He argued that America had the advantage of a common language, ethnic communities that either melted into the mainstream or learned to live with one another, or common cultural commitments. In the new nations of other continents, these problems had not yet been worked out, and the give-and-take of the political forum had not yet been worked through. Therefore it is possible that one-party governments, as in Tunisia, should be considered options immediately available and better than doctrinaire totalitarianism that could wreak greater havoc.

While the giants staggered about in their awkward moves, a Third World was born and grew. Associating the West with the colonial foot it was prying loose from its neck, beguiled by a utopian ideology, impressed by the industrial accomplishments of

Russia, the new nations gravitated toward the Marxist option, although not necessarily into the Communist camp. Niebuhr called the West to its responsibility for massive development aid so that these new countries could generate their own political forms and style free of old imperialisms of the right or left.

The British Way

The same ambiguity found in all human constructs he saw in colonialism. Niebuhr did allude, however, to an oft-forgotten creative dimension, citing the tutorial role of Great Britain as it disengaged from its colonialism and took part in the new entity, the Commonwealth. Thus an old imperialism as it liquidated its heritage planted the seeds for a new civil order. Of course, even this option was not without mixed motives; Britain saw the trade possibilities and other supports which would derive from it. For all that, Niebuhr always esteemed the British way, both in its pragmatic evolution of justice in internal affairs and its openness to change in external dealings with other nations. This esteem was symbolized by his acknowledgment of Churchill as the greatest statesman of the century, even with "Winnie's" sentimental attachment to the days of British hegemony as in his reluctance to end the British rule in India.

Unless the stalemate of nuclear horror fails, triggering the suicide of the race, the maneuvers and counter-maneuvers of the major powers are destined to be with us for years and perhaps centuries to come. They will be adjudicated, he held, at least in the foreseeable future, not by a utopian world government but by a wise statecraft. That statecraft will be moved both by the ideal of tolerable mutuality and by realism which takes into account collective egoisms and the attendant righteous pretensions of all the contenders for world power.

chapter 4

REALISM AND VISION

Toward the end of Niebuhr's life, a new breed of visionary was appearing. Political revolutionaries dreamt of a better world that drove them to call into question all that was, in the light of what might be. Neomystics experimented with an expanded consciousness which purported to see through and beyond drab and dreary commonplaces. Futurists spun out scenarios of the year 2000. Whatever form it took, vision began to nudge the absorption in the "now" and its visibilities. The "not yet" and the "can't-be-seen" exercised a new attraction.

Criticism of Niebuhr and his sober reminders of life's limitations came, predictably, from these visionaries. "Realism makes people afraid to walk on water!" declared an innovative spirit. Critics asserted that realism was so preoccupied with balancing power blocks and practicing the art of the possible that commitment to the needed radical social change was undercut. It lacked a passion for the future, for doing the undoable, thinking the unthinkable, seeing the unseen. The times called for revolutionary hope, not captivity to empirical givens, mesmerism with the ambiguities of the present, and compromising reformism. Life's possibilities, not sober realism about its impossibilities, were the order of the day.

Those dubious about realism pointed to the political timidity of some self-declared "Niebuhrians." Critics were also quick to note that prominent disciples of Niebuhr had little good to say about the New Left, political or ecclesiastical, nor were they often found in the front ranks of war protest and resistance. Further, the resources for Christian-Marxist dialogue in Niebuhrian thought seemed to be used more as ammunition for attack than as asserting some common concern about both realities and hopes. In short, visionaries found Christian realism to be a brake rather than a motor of political and religious forward movement.

Were the critics right? No, on two counts: (1) their understanding of Niebuhr's thought and (2) their failure to see how realism can and must be related to hope.

The Hidden Vision in Niebuhr

Contrary to the new utopians, Niebuhr's Christian realism is neither cynicism of the spirit nor political Machiavellianism. There *is* a vision of the future, the coming reign of God which is the lure and judge of all human attitudes and acts. Reflecting Reformed (leftwing Calvinist) sensibilities, Niebuhr often spoke of it in terms of the divine sovereignty as well as the Kingdom of perfect love and justice yet to be. Such a radical norm precludes opportunism, accommodation to the status quo, and conscienceless compromise. To practice the art of the politically possible does not erase the dream out ahead, a dream that constantly exerts its pull toward more imaginative goals and leaves one impatient with the status quo. And in that history short of the Kingdom's coming, there are what Niebuhr called "indeterminate possibilities." Such limitless advances, albeit always accompanied by their corruptibility, are thinkable because the image of God in humanity, though defaced, has not been obliterated. Further, the coming reign of God itself is at work in our midst as foretaste and earnest, though not as finale. And the mandate to pursue these possibilities is fortified by the assurance that God will complete our incompleteness at "the end of history." Thus the biblical visionary is saved from the despairs as well as the illusions of those who "have hope only in this life."

Vision Bashful, Realism Bold

The grounding of Niebuhr's political activism in biblical hope is buried deep in his writings, less visible in the widely read political commentary than in the sermonic and theological material. The overlay of popular interpretations which mined only the surface ore of his frequent reflection on history's ambiguities and corruptions needed to be penetrated. Also, in his period of greatest prominence, Niebuhr *did* accent the impossibilities rather than the possibilities of history. Indeed, it would have been obscene to talk about visions when nightmares were a reality in Belsen, Dachau, and Auschwitz, and when shattered dreams were a daily experience in an era of depression, totalitarianism, unchallenged racism, and global war.

In such times, the standard brand churches — called to be custodians of Christian realism — not only continued in the main to prattle about human goodness and upward progress but relied on programs of moral preachment or personal conversion to change demonic social structures and were innocent of their own self-righteous temptations. The harsh accents of a frowning Niebuhr, indicting utopianism, naivete, and the pretentious visionary, were the right notes to be sounded in that time of trouble and self-deception.

Vision Bold, Realism Bashful

What is to the foreground in one act of the human drama may not necessarily be so in another. In the 1960s, an era of rising expectations and determinations among those long submerged — the poor, the young, African Americans, women, new nations, consumers — a new forward momentum appeared with Martin Luther King Jr. as a symbol of those who "had a dream." In that same period an accelerating science technology, including dramatic biomedical advances, held out the promise of making real the age-old hopes of feeding the hungry, giving sight to the blind, hearing to the deaf, and enabling the lame to walk. Put these developments together with the growing realization that hopelessness is a self-fulfilling prophecy, and we can understand why many in our culture resonated with the aphorism given currency by Robert Kennedy: others dream of things that never were and ask "why not?"

While realism will mute its trumpets in an era of hope, it will not, it must not, be tuned out. As John Bennett put it in an important symposium on this issue, "Nothing has happened to refute the realistic analysis of the stubbornness of evil in society or the tragic side of history. No return to a pre-Niebuhrian optimism is possible."[1] Indeed, Martin King, the embodiment of the era's hopes and visions, acknowledged Niebuhr as one of his mentors. At what points, then, is the reminder of the "stubbornness of evil" a crucial component in a theology of hope making it a theology of sober hope?

1. John Bennett, in "Christian Realism: A Symposium," *Christianity and Crisis,* Vol. XXVIII, No. 14 (August 5, 1968), 176.

Contesting Entrenched Power

One of Niebuhr's most persistent theological New Left critics of that day, Richard Shaull, tacitly employed a Niebuhrian premise in his call for an antiestablishment coalition on the thesis that countervailing power was required. Corrupt and obsolete institutions are not changed by moral suasion but by counter-pressures, economic, social, and political. The human rights revolution of the sixties and beyond assumed the necessity of organizing the black community to wrest its freedom from autocracies and paternalisms, having no illusions about the effectiveness of reason and conscience alone to do the job. Thus in the era of revolt against old oligarchies, recognition of the stubbornness of entrenched power, its pretensions to virtue, and the need to muster compensating pressures was as fresh as ever. Niebuhr earlier had applied this realism to the confrontation of the worker with industrial baronies and to the battle against totalitarianism; it re-emerged in these subsequent moments of social change.

Succeeding decades brought the need for new waves of marginalized people to organize. Realism recognized that hierarchies and autocracies do not relinquish control by appeals to conscience. Indeed, society, as such, must protect itself from monolithic decision-making by dispersing its power, allowing "the weak things of the world and the despised" to press their case through collective means.

The church itself is not exempt from the temptations of power. Where hegemony is exercised by privileged groups in its own ranks, the voiceless must find their own voice. Thus, the "base communities" in Latin America, women organizing their own support and dissent groups, laity asserting the legitimacy of their ministry, pastors challenging bureaucracies, and evangelical parachurch movements are a few manifestations of ecclesial realism.

Temptations of Ascending Power

Talk of our universal "sin" is anathema to visionary activists. They hold that the problem is not our common sin before God but the plight of the "sinned-against." Homilies on the pride and mixed motives of the committed and the ambiguities of history are sand thrown in the machines of social change. We should focus on history's hopes and opportunities, not its tainted motives and dangerous shoals.[2]

Early American revolutionaries felt the same righteous indignation about English hegemony, and pulpits provided their full share of theological accreditation for colonial resistance. However, those same revolutionaries, with insight into the corruptibility of power, including their own newly acquired power, built into the structures of governance legislative, executive, and judicial checks and balances. Latter-day American reformers and revolutionaries need this same kind of sobriety about the dangers of unrestrained power. The forces of dissent in every time and place are subject to the corruptions that threaten historical advance. Thus the Christian conscience must play its classical role of participant critic; it gives its heart to the movement for social change, but not its soul. Deeply involved, it nonetheless maintains its freedom to dissent. Supporting the forward surge, it provides both accelerator and brake, applying each when the time calls for it.

An example of this kind of "yes, but" relationship to emerging power is the partnership the Christian community can establish with biological revolutionaries. There had better be some sober Niebuhrians at the council tables of biotechnicians who decide

2. See Harvey G. Cox, *On Not Leaving It to the Snake* (New York: The Macmillan Company, 1968), especially vii-xviii.

policy on the creation, control, extension, and termination of human life. Christian realists will have on their agenda the goal of affirming the right of those whose lives will be affected by these developments, especially having those of "low degree" represented in the decision-making processes.

Sobered Expectations

We have been dwelling so far on realism's estimate of the vulnerability of power, and the need for balancing inordinate expressions of it. But there is a broader application, much used by Niebuhr in counsel to his contemporaries about what tomorrow may bring. Do not expect the Kingdom to come in history. Evil grows with good. (One of his well-known sermons takes as text the parable of the wheat and the tares — Matt. 13:24-30). The anti-Christ appears in the last days. In this rich metaphor Niebuhr saw the ambiguity of all historical achievement.

Because of the high visibility of totalitarianisms, tragic wars, and depressions in his time, Niebuhr put stress on the evil that persists as society advances; it can easily be forgotten, as we have noted, that he also pointed to history's possibilities. Humanity *can* hope for the correction of specific abuses that mar a given period. Within Niebuhr's framework, King did indeed have a right to dream that black and white children would walk the streets together in peace.

But Niebuhr reminded us about the illusions we court at every level of historical advance. Each terrain is mined. Further, sobriety entails self-criticism. To be schooled in Niebuhr is to know that our plans and projects are infected with our private agendas and molded by our historical location. For Niebuhr, such soul-searching is grounded in eschatology as well as anthropology.

History moves toward its finale. Nothing is solidly nailed down. Thus we are suspicious of our pretensions to finality, taking them with a certain good humor.

Violence and Nonviolence

Is Niebuhr's criticism of pacifism still valid? Yes, but Christian realism must take into account the new contexts in which it finds itself. (The latter sensitivity to changing circumstances is "realism" in the more general sense: acknowledgment of the realities of the situation. Awareness of context is the pragmatic factor in Niebuhrian thought. We have used the term "realism" throughout in the narrower sense: acknowledging the reality of a stubborn evil that persists in human will, behavior, and social structures.) New contexts include increasing availability of nuclear weaponry to paramilitary units within nations, to criminal syndicates, and to emerging nations with their bursting of colonial bonds and resistance to neocolonialism, and the growing importance in domestic struggles of tactical and moral questions having to do with nonviolence, defensive violence, and aggressive violence. The following seem to be some implications in the light of post-Niebuhrian realities:

1. Given the nuclear arsenal of the major powers and the possible imminent acquisition of comparable resources by other nations, the chance of atomic holocaust becomes even more of a possibility. Adding a particularly fearful dimension to this prospect is the accidental triggering of a nuclear Armageddon. Here realism and vision meet. Sinful humanity with this kind of awesome power in its hands can only be dealt with by concerted counter-efforts in peacemaking. That means a nuclear

pacifism which, at the very least, calls for radical mutual disarmament proposals and action. Post-Niebuhrian realists can no longer rest comfortably with balance-of-terror theories.

2. Many realists marched in the same demonstrations as ideological pacifists because they agreed with Niebuhr about the Vietnam War. Where the strange mix of American arrogance and innocence occurs as it did in that war — with its political miscalculations and coldblooded militarism — realists will join forces with visionaries.

3. A sober hope will not erase realism's hardheaded acknowledgment of the role of violence in international affairs. Given "immoral man and even more immoral society," a military component will be necessary for the foreseeable future in the settlement of world problems. It should be voluntarized, democratized, and internationalized (a U.N. peacekeeping force), its instruments stringently limited (the outlawing of chemical and biological as well as nuclear warfare), strict canons developed on the treatment of civilians, and all these restraints and changes given machinery of enforcement. The employment of military power for humanitarian purposes and the restraint of tyranny under international auspices, for all its ambiguities, has demonstrated its importance in the 1990s.

4. So far we have been dealing with international conflict. What of tyranny within a nation as in the Revolution of 1776 and the struggles for human dignity in the autocratic regimes of the 1990s? The collapse of Marxist societies through nonviolent protest movements demonstrates once again the power of vision cum organization in social change. This must be the working norm of realistic visionaries. Yet when all the methods of peaceful change have been exhausted and a resolute tyranny remains, an exception to the nonviolent rule is conceivable. At such a historical moment, the Christian com-

mitment of realism and vision must pray for the gift of discernment among competing evils and for forgiveness of sin.

Day-to-day issues of violence confront us in the barroom, kitchen, bedroom, hospital, and hunting lodge. They are omnipresent in inner city and suburbia, town and country. They have to do with gun laws, police treatment of minorities, anxiety about criminal assault, the battering of women, the abuse of children. Here vision and realism embrace. What is ultimately good — the dignity of persons in the final realm of God — is also realistically fit in a society that does not come asunder.

Sober Hope

Hope can never be severed from reality in matters both secular and ecclesial. Yet somewhere, somehow, as Niebuhr himself affirmed, there must be a small cadre of those who steward visions. Such a community of conscience reminds us that anything less than the Kingdom is short of God's final intent for the world. It forces us to realize that our translations, qualifications, and scaling down of this ultimate dream of perfection always stand under the judgment of standards held up by the historically marginal perfectionist.

For the rest of us who cannot or choose not to live along the edges of historical ambiguity, but who believe nonetheless that *shalom* is the ultimate norm, the way ahead entails dialectical dreaming and marching in the ranks of "sober hopers." While pressing toward the Goal, they know they must settle regularly for less. Yet they live by hope rather than hopelessness, the word of the grace that meets sin, the resurrection that follows crucifixion.

chapter 5

NIEBUHRIAN COUNSELS
AND CORRECTIVES

Visionary realism by no means exhausts the Niebuhrian bequest to the future. The legacy runs from somber warnings for the smug and complacent to insights on laughter for the dour and depressed. It ranges over counsel for the left and the right, the church and the world, the mystic and the secular. All the promissory motifs in this assorted wisdom go back to basic Niebuhrian postulates about humanity and God.

Niebuhr was no all-wise guru, as he was the first to admit. Some of his notions were mistaken, askew, dated. Critics he had aplenty. Therefore, in good Niebuhrian style we shall first attend to the perils of our subject. Then, befitting a partisan on "the promise of Reinhold Niebuhr," we shall find more to celebrate than denigrate.

It is not hard to find critics and criticism. They surfaced irately in the wake of his attacks on the illusions of modern humanity. Each target of his lightning hurled back his own bolts. Marxists accused him of being an apologist for capitalism. The right wing called him a communist. Naturalists declared that he wallowed in religious superstition. Idealists asserted that he sold out to irrationalism. Pacifists bewailed his compromise with the absolutes of love. Cynics claimed that he confused action with his high principles. Orthodox Christians labeled him an unbeliever who failed to hew the line on everything from the divinity of Christ and the resurrection to the doctrine of the Holy Spirit. The church-minded felt he ignored the institution, or criticized it too much. The worldly said he was too churchy. The pious declared that he was too political. The political said he was too pious.

Amid the wild charges against Niebuhr, there were some that did strike home. His doctrine of the church was undeveloped, and his place for the Holy Spirit was indeed minimal. He was not a systematic theologian. Neither was he a painstaking philosopher. His tendency to portray options in broad brush strokes caused him to classify the opposition too easily and dismiss it too brusquely. He made some serious political miscalculations. Limitations acknowledged, attention here is turned to some of Niebuhr's durable wisdom, especially as it relates both to the specifics of twentieth-century challenges and perennial human quandaries.

The Love of God for God's Own Sake

Niebuhr remarked from time to time upon the paradox that the most productive things often come not by prudence and calculation but as if by happenstance. He believed this kind of heedlessness to be at the center of Christian belief. The central understandings in Christian faith about humanity can be appropriated only by self-abandonment and penitence. Faith is not heavenly hedonism but the love of God for God's own sake. This "for its own sake" dimension is important in an era of secularization. The truth of our fundamental convictions and commitments does not finally rest on its pragmatic value. Through and beyond its usefulness to the human struggle — a test that must always remain in order to disqualify claims which cannot produce ethical fruits — can be seen a glimpse of a friendship with God that is not justified by utility. It is simply there to be had. God is to be loved for God's own sake.

Sensitive young people, expressing their revulsion with empirical, pragmatic, secular society, its technogical horrors and calculating egoism, flirt with the Oriental and the esoteric. Niebuhr noted the periodic slide of rationalism into mysticism. We may well be seeing that rhythm once again. His warnings about the possibility of anti-intellectualism and a retreat inward and away from historical responsibility in such a swing of the pendulum have to be taken seriously. However, in this shift there is an authentic judgment on the life of self-interested calculation, the hypocrisies of an affluent society, and a sound instinct for the inscrutable, too easily exorcised by a cocksure scientism. And Niebuhr himself spoke movingly of mystery as integral to faith, taking to task in his day the insensitivity of the death-of-God theologians to this dimension. Perhaps talk of a life with God which has no agenda may find resonance among those who search for deeper things.

Humor and Faith

Celebration, play, humor, and laughter were rediscovered in the religious community. Christ grinned out from the illustration of a *Playboy* article by Harvey Cox, who argued there, and in the *Feast of Fools,* the importance of festivity and fantasy. Others pled *For God's Sake, Laugh!* and brought together anthologies of *Holy Laughter.* The mood was reflected in celebrative worship that made full use of the sounds of folk and rock, the sights of banners, balloons, and multimedia techniques, and smells of incense.[1]

Well before the accents on play, celebration, and fantasy that emerged in the 1960s, when sobriety was the order of the day in both worship and theology, Reinhold Niebuhr was reminding us that the God "who sits in the heavens laughs" (Ps. 2:4). In some reflections of the mid-1940s, widely read and reprinted, he explored the kinship between humor and faith. What he had to say about that relationship probes it more deeply than much later comment on the religious significance of drollery.

Hope and joy blend as they did in the art of Corita Kent. Theologies of hope were associated with festive color and celebrative sound. Niebuhr too, as an ultimate hoper (a submerged motif as we have noted, given the historical context of his labors), also spoke of a joy commensurate with the final overcoming of the power of evil and, in individual terms, "on the other side of the experience of penitence." But faith strikes its note of triumph (Niebuhr thought of it more often as serenity than gaiety) only after passing through a shadowy valley. The note of crucifixion of self, society, and God was often missing in the sixties theologies of play and celebration. The same absence is notable in liturgical counterparts. "Is folk music stuck on a single note?" asked a perceptive critic who found many efforts at contemporary worship lacking in depth and verging on the sentimental.[2]

Niebuhr had a sharp eye for profundities and found laughter

1. See Harvey G. Cox, *The Feast of Fools* (Cambridge: Harvard University Press, 1969), Nevin Vos, *For God's Sake, Laugh!* (Richmond: John Knox Press, 1967), M. Conrad Hyers, ed., *Holy Laughter* (New York: The Seabury Press, 1969).

2. "Is Folk Music Stuck on a Single Note?" *National Catholic Reporter,* Vol. 6, No. 8 (December 17, 1969), 1, 7.

helpless to deal with them. The depths of our own self-will and the heights of our pretension, the incongruity of death, the malice that exterminates six million Jews are no laughing matter. In the end, only penitence, faith, and sacrificial love are fit responses. Laughter in the face of these realities is "gallows humor," bitter and self-defeating. Yet in the penultimate moment, the joke that ridicules the high and mighty — that allows an ordinary person to mock behavior that hurts — yields a momentary freedom from persecution, saving the daily routine from grinding harrassment. The numbers of jokes circulated during the decades of the Cold War testify to the cleansing quality of stepping almost to the edge of danger, believing oneself to be right, but stating the outrageous as humor which cannot quite indict the speaker. It almost begs God to be an ally. It gathers round it, almost in fellowship, those who can appreciate the joke and are not too afraid to laugh. Such courage can come close to describing the mature person whom God wills us to be.

One of the deeper dimensions is the mystery of the divine life and action, manifest centrally in the cross. Although direct quotation has been purposely avoided in this volume in the interests of a free-flowing interpretation of the promissory, a memorable passage illustrates the point under discussion and also uncovers a basic theological foundation in Niebuhr's thought.

> There is . . . no humour in the scene of Christ upon the cross
> . . . because the justice and mercy of God are fully revealed in
> it. In that revelation God's justice is made the more terrible
> because the sin of man is disclosed in its full dimension. It is
> rebellion against God from which God Himself suffers. God
> cannot remit the consequences of sin; yet He does show
> mercy by taking the consequences upon and into Himself.

This is the main burden of the disclosure of God in Christ. This is the final clue to the mystery of the divine character.[3]

Faith alone can deal with the ultimate mysteries. But there is plenty of room for laughter in dealing with the sickness of petty self-inflation. A sense of humor teaches not to take ourselves so seriously. The same laughter is proper judgment on the pretensions of others. Both we and they fail to see the incongruity between our conceits and our mediocrity. Laughter is a good resource in coming to terms with many other juxtapositions with which we must learn to live, such as the unpredictable events that intrude upon our well-laid plans, and the irrationalities that mar our dreams.

The kinship between humor and faith lies precisely at the point of dealing with the incongruities of our life, our pretension and our performance, our sublime expectations and the modest and often fractured realities, our greatness and our weakness. Laughter plays its role in dealing with these ill fits, as does faith. Their jurisdictions and interrelationship are set forth in a simple passage that illustrates not only an insight but also the kind of purple patch to be found not infrequently in this powerful writer: "there is laughter in the vestibule of the temple, the echo of laughter in the temple itself, but only faith and prayer, and no laughter, in the holy of holies."[4]

Advice for the Right and the Left

Niebuhr's running battle with political and religious reactionaries of another day offers many lessons. Warnings about the pride of na-

3. Reinhold Niebuhr, "Humour and Faith," in *Discerning the Signs of the Times* (New York: Charles Scribner's Sons, 1946), 118-19.
4. Niebuhr, "Humour and Faith," 131.

tion, race, and class are anything but obsolete. Militarism and chauvinism ally themselves today with a confused idealism to wage war, support military juntas, and resist movements for reform on several continents. Meanwhile the same forces harass and imprison the dissenter. Racism, cut from the same cloth as old blood-and-soil philosophies, gains momentum in south and north, at home and abroad. A conscienceless majority strives to protect its affluence, resists programs for the poverty-ridden, and greets the lament of the urban poor with its cries of "law and order."

These are familiar sounds. They have to do with themes vigorously underscored by Niebuhr: the ubiquity of self-regard, its demonic compounding in the theater of historical forces, its special arrogance among the powerful, and the self-righteous smokescreen which proud power always lays down around itself. Out of this comes the mandate, as fresh as ever, to challenge, disperse, and balance the imperialisms of the right.

The political right is matched in its pretension by the religious right. In fact, the two become partners in a new civil religion. The union is so firm that an old pietism that drew back from involvement in politics baptizes the programs of the powers-that-be, dispenses absolution for their conscience. Niebuhr's misgivings about an earlier Billy Graham and Norman Vincent Peale, declared in the midst of the postwar religious boom, were expressed again at the outset of "the Nixon era," and spoken to us again in the era of popular television evangelists. They will have perennial significance whenever a religion of cheap grace provides cover for political reaction.

The left as well as the right need to hear a word that shakes their certainties and presumed righteousness. Niebuhr's realism about entrenched power supports the struggles of the oppressed. Yet their motives may also be mixed and their acquisition of power is not impervious to corruption. In this chapter attention will be given to Niebuhrian counsel to a range of political activists and cultural critics.

The Minutes of the Last Meeting

Niebuhr believed, in the words of a college chaplain, that "we can avoid a lot of nonsense by reading the minutes of the last meeting." Much of his political analysis was fashioned from the data of the past. A generation that is mesmerized by the present throws away one of its most valuable tools for social change. The present is no simple repetition of the "once upon a time," but neither is it discontinuous with it. Niebuhr understood historical novelty but was aware as well of historical continuities, and harnessed this understanding to the task of political action. An expression of the theological left innocent of last meeting's minutes is situation ethics. Its defenders attacked Niebuhr for his "ontological" absolutes, arguing instead for an existential ethic free of remorse for standards breached.

Niebuhr affirmed an eschatological standard by which all our lesser motives, actions, and structures must be judged, and toward which they must aspire, albeit under the limiting conditions of sin and finitude. To remove this ultimate Ought against which we measure ourselves censors the final chapter in the Christian story and denies the reality of guilt, *coram Deo*. Thus, the case of the British intelligence staff in World War II: "When they let a number of women agents return to Germany to certain arrest and death in order to keep secret the fact that they had broken the German code, situational casuistry could easily approve their decision."[5] (Or when Churchill knowingly sacrificed

5. Joseph Fletcher, *Situation Ethics* (Philadelphia: Westminster Press, 1966), 98.

Coventry for the same reason.) Here, the Niebuhr who refuses to eliminate the transhistorical norm rejects the equation of what must be done with what is ultimately right. Choices less than the sacrificial love of the Kingdom are not decisions we ought "easily approve." With his friend, Bonhoeffer, who chose to plot against Hitler's life and prayed for forgiveness, Niebuhr knew that they are *hard* choices, made in fear and trembling, in penitence for the evil done, even a "lesser" evil, and with a plea for divine mercy. So, too, the decision-maker is driven to work all the harder toward a world in which fewer such choices have to be made.

The existential Now surely must affect our decision-making. But this slender moment of time does not exhaust the data. Realism is well aware of the distortions introduced by that limited immediate perspective, and aggravated by its self-interest. We need others present at the councils of decision — both elders and contemporaries. Wisdom comes from the historic experience of the race and from the research done by the covenant community in which the decision-maker lives. The rugged individualism and exclusive present-orientation of situation ethics must be corrected by the community's moral lore, history's wisdom, and a corporate way of decision-making.

No one is an island. Moral decision-making must be made somewhere in range of the mainland of human community and, for the Christian, also within the faith community. To take the community into serious account includes, of course, the present task of updating and translating, the development of "middle axioms" on questions for which there is no historic research; moral quandaries about the creation, control, and indefinite extension of human life now on the drawing board and even in the laboratories of the life sciences require this kind of corporate quest.

Theological Method

Liberation action-reflection theologies assert the role of *praxis* in "doing theology." Field education pioneers stress reflection in the context of involvement. Long before these current accents, Niebuhr lived out his own "action-reflection" rhythm. One of the British thinkers influenced by Niebuhr, Alexander Miller, who walked his own picket lines in the thirties and forties, put it this way: "The safest place for the theologian is in the midst of the social struggle."

One of the ironies in the life of our irony-conscious subject is his frequent disclaimer that he is really not a theologian because of his preoccupation with social change, and his apology that he should have spent more time at his desk and less in political movements. Yet Niebuhr's radical critique of perfectionism — his understanding of pride, ambiguity and idolatry, Old Testament prophetism, the need for forgiveness, the meaning of the cross, the reality of the hidden Christ — is directly related to his participation in the crunch of political and social life.

The Secular Dialogue

From his first confrontations with Marx and Freud to his review of the latest book on political thought or psychological theory, Niebuhr carried on an appreciative yet critical conversation with non-ecclesiastical thought. The powerful of the human community, as well as some less influential ones, too, were not just set up as targets for thunderbolts he lobbed from on high (he surely hurled his share), but as partners whose insights were to be taken seriously on the intellectual pilgrimage and honored for their truth.

In his later writing Niebuhr accented his debt to secular

thought. And he attempted to translate more simply into general human categories some of his understandings about human nature and destiny. These themes are highlighted in *Man's Nature and His Communities,*[6] but there are traces of this honoring of general revelation and "the covenant with Noah" from the beginning of his career. God raises up children of Abraham from secular stones.

The Christian Story

While books of sermons have a diminishing audience, Niebuhr's collections (*Beyond Tragedy*[7] and *Discerning the Signs of the Times*[8]) are still avidly read. In these volumes, but also in his more scholarly works and even in his political editorials, Old and New Testament passages often provided the springboard for reflection. Niebuhr took the Christian story seriously. Political involvement, yes; secular sensitivity, yes. But each such commitment was acknowledged because of its authorization by biblical faith. Indeed his dramatic-historical interpretation of the Gospel anticipated a later narrative theology.

The Storybook

Life with the Christian story means at least two basic things. For one, familiarity with Scripture. Niebuhr did his theology in conversation with the biblical text. Millions of Sunday morning wor-

6. Reinhold Niebuhr, *Man's Nature and His Communities* (New York: Scribner's, 1965; Lanham, Md.: University Press of America, 1988).

7. Reinhold Niebuhr, *Beyond Tragedy* (New York: Charles Scribner's Sons, 1937; New York: The Macmillan Company, 1979).

8. Reinhold Niebuhr, *Discerning the Signs of the Times* (New York: Charles Scribner's Sons, 1946).

shipers during the forties and fifties were called to honest self-examination and reminded, as well, of "the laughter of God." Unknown texts became familiar fare through a generation of preaching influenced by Niebuhrian insights.

Conversation with the Bible is not biblicism. Niebuhr was accused of that sometimes by agnostic friends whose only exposure to faith was the Bible-thumping radio evangelist. His biblical thunder sounded similar, but careful listeners were aware of the critical scholarship through which the storybook had passed to get at the substance. But more important, what really interested Niebuhr in his expositions were the biblical narratives. Here were the nuggets. They had to be refined to get the gold, of course — that's what Niebuhr's preaching and teaching were all about. The truth about the ambiguity of the human condition, the corruptions of the good, and the possibilities of history were traced out in the Genesis account, the Babel tale, and the death and resurrection of Christ.

The Storytellers

It is possible to be absorbed in the storyline of the Book but pay little attention to other storytellers, the second crucial way the word gets out. That is our Protestant problem. Not so Niebuhr. He drew the conversation circle wide enough to include the church's fathers and mothers, brothers and sisters. Niebuhr listened to and argued with Augustine, Luther, Aquinas, Kierkegaard. They found their way into many a footnote which provided more scrupulous professional historians a chance to comment on Niebuhr's use or misuse of his sources, all of which widened the dialogue even further.

Niebuhr's exchanges with contemporary Christian thinkers went on concurrently with the classical theologians. Participation in the World Council of Churches and its predecessor ecumenical agencies brought him into debate with the giants of his time. We have spoken about the sharp exchange with Barth at the 1948 Assembly. His colleagues on the Union faculty, such as John Bennett and Paul Tillich, offered him a constant chance to sharpen his insights. And his wide-ranging speaking tours brought him into contact with the keenest theological minds of the day. Christian realism was not eremite theology. It was shaped by a life together in the theological guild, and within a larger Christian community.

Courage to Change

This title of June Bingham's biography of Niebuhr, taken from his famous prayer, expresses yet another determining characteristic: an openness to the future.[9] One of the marks of a great theologian is the capacity to develop, at the painful price of admitting mistakes, abandoning old categories, moving along new frontiers.

An allied quality of a responsive theologian is the ability to discern the signs of the times and speak the right word in and to these times. When the Nazi era pleaded for a prophetic indictment and a shattering of sentimental illusions, Niebuhr spoke that word. When a pietism that professed knowledge of human sin retreated from the structures of the common life, it was Niebuhr who unleashed his thunderbolts — as with the rebuke of Billy Graham (while many in the officialdom of the church acclaimed his New York campaign). When social-action types collapsed the Gospel into an attack on economic and political struc-

9. June Bingham, *The Courage to Change: An Introduction to the Life and Thought of Reinhold Niebuhr* (New York: Scribner, 1972).

tures, he spoke about the need for prayer and the broken self. When "secularism" became a favorite denigration, Niebuhr underscored the common grace at work in non-ecclesiastical persons and movements. When secular theology took up its refrain, he reminded its adherents of mystery and myth and the grandeur of God. In each of these cases, Niebuhr's thought moves away from theses with which he had become too neatly associated. But while he was prepared to abandon positions found untenable, he also maintained commitments he believed to be of continuing significance.

The courage to change makes for a pilgrim theology. But the traveler must carry a well-stocked pack. Its supplies include provender prepared by others who have gone before and know the sustenance needed for unmarked trails. The pilgrimage goes forward, open to the future but fortified by the past.

chapter 6

PROMISES FULFILLED: THE 1990s

" Reinhold Niebuhr's Long Shadow . . ." So the *New York Times* titled Arthur Schlesinger Jr.'s 1992 op-ed tribute to Niebuhr's lasting significance. Schlesinger wrote:

> He persuaded me and many of my contemporaries that original sin provides a far stronger foundation for freedom and self-government than illusions about human perfectibility. . . . His warnings against utopianism, messianism, and perfectionism strike a chord today. We are beginning to remember what we should never have forgotten: we cannot play the role of God to history, and we must strive as best we can to attain decency, clarity, and proximate justice in an ambiguous world.[1]

The prescience of Niebuhr's political wisdom can be matched by the durability of its theological foundations, both remarked upon by Schlesinger. In this twenty-three-year update chapter written for the revised edition of this book, primary attention shall be given to the latter with implications for the former noted.

1. *New York Times*, June 22, 1992, A17.

Revisiting the Visionaries

Advocates of the "theology of revolution" as well as the softer utopians of the counter-culture who attacked Niebuhr's Christian realism in the 1960s, interlocutors in the first edition of this book, are long gone. Also, exponents of one or another liberation theology who faulted Niebuhr for his stress upon original sin have had to re-examine their own inordinate claims for both Marxist analysis and the societies shaped by it. While history has refuted these critics, other movements and interpretations have continued what we have earlier identified as the visionary impulse. Indeed, some have chosen Niebuhr as their special target. To demonstrate the enduring importance of Niebuhr's political and ethical thought, we survey some end-of-the-century variations on "utopianism, messianism, and perfectionism."

Political Fundamentalism

From the late 1970s to the present, right-wing religious cum political passions and movements have had a significant impact on American society. While pluralistic in nature (for example, the Moral Majority included varied religious traditions; thus it was called the "religious right" rather than the "Christian right"), primary impetus has come from the fundamentalist wing of Protestant evangelicalism.[2] Following the fall of some of its television titans at the end of the 1980s, and the demise of the Moral Majority, popular commentary declared the movement to be

2. For the writer's description and assessment of this phenomenon, see his *The Religious Right and Christian Faith* (Grand Rapids: Eerdmans Publishing Co., 1982) and "Political Fundamentalism" in *Theology, Politics and Peace*, ed. Theodore Runyon (Maryknoll: Orbis Books, 1989), 117-25.

over. However, the emergence of "The Christian Coalition," the zeal of the pro-life "Operation Rescue," and the various forays of Pat Robertson — his presidential campaign, the creation of the cable "Family Channel," the effort to purchase a major wire service, and the organization of The Christian Coalition itself — contradict the obituaries. A Niebuhrian cultural analysis and theological assessment can help us understand its persistence and address its dangers.

Both religious and political visionary movements appeal to a capacity of the human spirit — the intact aspect of the *imago Dei* — to envisage history's "indeterminate possibilities." In Christian elaborations, eschatological hope portrays a world of absolute freedom and peace. Political fundamentalism is a variation of evangelicalism taken to the political arena, the "born again" experience giving a present taste of eschatological salvation. Zealous efforts are made to establish on earth signs of the arriving reign of God, a political "new birth." When an apocalyptic timetable is added, the pressures intensify to prepare the way for the soon-coming King. Again, as an evangelical movement that stresses personal virtues, the political agenda focuses on issues of private morality interpreted through a literalist reading of Scripture (a conservative version of "inerrancy"), hence the high profile of "family values" and campaigns against abortion and homosexuality.

Niebuhr's Christian realism, as has been argued earlier, had its own visionary component, and thus had room for the claims of the Not Yet on the fallen Now. His appreciation of left-wing Reformation movements and political Calvinism suggests that he would recognize and respect the intention of political fundamentalism to make its witness in the public arena and thus constitute an advance over the apolitical pietism he regularly criticized. His own conception of sexuality and affirmation of the marriage covenant, as in his criticism of the naturalism of the Kinsey report, would give a sympathetic ear to parallel concerns in the religious right. However, in the end, he would indict the political fundamentalists for the breach of their own professed Christian commitments.

Missing in both its theology and its practice is a biblical understanding of sin. By extending into the political arena the sharp "born again" disjunction between the saved and the unsaved, the world is divided up sharply between "us" and "them." While this generates impressive political passion (paralleling the evangelistic zeal that rises from evangelical piety), it also provides no principle of self-criticism for "the righteous" and no appreciation of the positive elements in the positions of the "unrighteous." Political fundamentalism is innocent of the ambiguities of the political order, especially the sin that persists in the ranks of the "redeemed." As such, it is easily subject to the corruptibility that attends power, whether that power be political, economic, moral, or spiritual. The pyramiding of authority with no internal checks and balances, and no piety of self-criticism, led predictably to the abuse of "money, sex, and power" in the empires of various television evangelists. Political fundamentalists with no doctrine of continuing sin in the souls or structures of the sanctified will always be prey to the twin tendencies identified by Niebuhr: self-righteous fury and unrealistic expectations, on the one hand, and on the other, despair and retreat from involvement when these inordinate self-definitions are confounded by the facts.

Neoconservatism

Leading theological figures in theo-political neoconservatism have regular recourse to Niebuhrian analysis. However, vindicated by the collapse of communist societies, some declare for alternative economic and political theories with a zeal reminiscent of Marxist absolutisms. Michael Novak, while disavowing the identification of any temporal system with the Kingdom of God, urges trust in the historical processes that brought capitalism to be (Adam Smith's "invisible hand") — along with its release of human creativities and communities of conscience to monitor its possible excesses. In a similar vein, George Weigel points to the working of Providence in history to bring to be the inherent goodness of an "American experiment" with the promise now in our unipolar world of an era of "pax Americana."[3]

Niebuhr would certainly make a case for democratic societies. However, the confidences expressed by neoconservatives in selected processes of history — capitalist and American — and the virtues they are presumed to evoke, carry with them little sense of the ambiguities of both human creativity and communities of conscience. Niebuhr's anthropology and theology of history would sharply question the semi-Pelagian assumptions implicit in these analyses and forecasts. Warnings are here in order about the attractions of ideology and the need for more pragmatic counsels. Missing is a healthy regard for the corruptibility of our finest heritage and most exalted visions.

Neopacifism

For some current ethicists, Niebuhr is the most influential representative of a "mainstream ethical consensus" that replaces with human strategies the New Testament witness to the *social* teaching of Jesus (presumed to be considered by Niebuhrians irrele-

3. A distillation of these points of view, along with those of other neoconservatives and their critics, can be found in Richard John Neuhaus and George Weigel, eds., *Being Christian Today: An American Conversation* (Washington, D.C.: Ethics and Public Policy Center, 1992).

vant to systemic questions).[4] By making this replacement, the "consensus" has allowed cultural ideologies to erode the unique identity of both the "Jesus story" and the Christian community. Faithfulness calls for recovery in the church of a language and behavior conformed to Christ and a willingness to live in the fallen world as "resident aliens." The retrieval of Christian distinctives means both rejection of the gods of war and the espousal of a countercultural pacifism lived without calculating the benefits of nonviolence and ready to suffer the consequences.

Where this view identifies itself as a form of "narrative theology,"[5] Niebuhr would recognize a kinship with his own effort in "biblical theology." Both employ the scriptural storyline as a theological framework, although for Niebuhr the stories at the christological center on which neopacifism focuses are placed within the larger drama that runs from creation to consummation with important places for the covenants with Noah ("general revelation") and Israel ("special revelation" in the law and the prophets). Further, Niebuhr's commentary on "drama," "myth," and "symbol" has affinities with the stress in various narrative theologies on the dynamisms of plot in the ways of God and the evocative power of story.

A Niebuhrian critique of narrative neopacifism would affirm its visionary commitments (contrary to simplistic readings of his Christian realism) and assert a role within the church for a pacifist subcommunity as witness to the eschatological standards by which all behavior must be judged. However, like conventional pacifism, this point of view has not integrated into its anthropol-

4. See John Howard Yoder, *The Politics of Jesus* (Grand Rapids: Eerdmans Publishing Co., 1972).

5. For a running critique of Niebuhr by an ethicist of this persuasion, see Stanley Hauerwas's comments in Richard John Neuhaus, ed., *Reinhold Niebuhr Today* (Grand Rapids: Eerdmans Publishing Co., 1989), 112-16 and *passim*.

ogy the Pauline teaching about the depth of sin. It thus fails to grasp the continuing power of egotism in the believer, the Christian community, and the wider world. The result is a perfectionist ethic that does not draw upon the wisdom available in either the covenant with Noah ("general revelation") or the covenant with Israel (the law and the prophets) for ways to achieve a tolerable social justice and viable approximations of eschatological goals. Needed as well is a church with the indicatives of mercy as well as the imperatives of righteousness for sinners who must live with these ambiguities. Further, the assertion that a perfectionist ethic is livable by the true believer, with the enemy "out there" in the camps of violence, masks the sin that persists in the life of the sanctified and begets a sectarian ecclesiology of "us and them."

The New Age Movement

Much like its gnostic antecedents, the New Age Movement is more an atmosphere than an identifiable theological perspective. Nevertheless, it has some common premises that link it with *fin de siècle* visionary themes. Whatever form it takes — "transformation training," philosophical cum mystical cosmology, lifestyle programs, or occult practice — New Ageism holds that the delusions inflicted upon us by Western culture and its religions can be eliminated by a new consciousness of unity with undifferentiated Reality. All that is is one, and this All is God. Our metaphysical amnesia can be corrected by monistic and pantheistic teaching implemented through techniques of meditation and mind-altering that include not only ancient arts from the Far East but also the resources of psycho-technology. In the popular idiom of a New Age advocate: "We are gods and might as well get good at it." Our journey in self-definition continues in subsequent reincarnate worlds until final spiritual deformations are eliminated and unity of both knowing and being is realized.

Niebuhr would be sympathetic with New Age concerns about the erosion of human dignity under the impact of modernity. So, too, the goodness of the natural order as the creation of God argues for the stewardship of the body and the animal and environmental sensitivity for which many New Age advocates are known. His pragmatism would allow for eclectic use of whatever whale and waterfall sounds or natural medical methods that make for "the serenity to accept" or the "courage to change."

A Niebuhrian critique of New Age theology and spirituality would turn to both biblical faith and discernible fact. Scripture, as interpreted in classical theology, teaches that creation is good, but not God, to be affirmed but not worshiped. Human nature made in the divine image is not to be fused with nature and, as creaturely, not to be confused with deity. The New Age premise that humanity is deity, and its program to encourage such a consciousness, is a window into the soul of modern narcissism and an expression of the root sin of idolatry. Predictably, talk of sin is considered anathema in New Age theory and practice (and is challenged as an Augustinian corruption in the kindred "original blessing" emphasis of Matthew Fox).[6] The elimination of original sin as a chapter in the human story is itself a form of delusion that invites misreading our imperial inclinations and our capacity for self-deception. The attendant moralism knows nothing of the message of justification by faith alone and the Good News of divine mercy. The spectacle of wealthy New Age movie stars legitimating their status as the result of a karmic trajectory of good works from a previous life and assuring liberation for those in personal or historical pain through consciousness-altering techniques is an odious example.

6. Matthew Fox, *Original Blessing* (Santa Fe: Bear & Co., 1983).

Feminism

Niebuhr's theology has come under critical scrutiny by religious feminists. Judith Plaskow, building on work by Valerie Saiving, developed a widely accepted critique of Niebuhr's anthropology.[7] Plaskow argues that the "pride" Niebuhr declared to be our universal sin is indeed the propensity of the wielders of power, manifest in the personal and political corruptions of the patriarchal society which surrounded him and the right target of his polemic. However, he mistakenly universalized the pride of the powerful as the sin to which all humanity fundamentally succumbs. While recognizing "sensuality" as a companion form of sin that fits the symmetry of his doctrine of human nature — our freedom as prey to pride and our creatureliness as subject to "sensuality" or the escape from freedom — he derived the latter from the former and tended to reduce it to "lust." Niebuhr's analysis is faulty and must be corrected by women's experience. In this culture, their problem is not "pride" but the refusal to assert their identity in the face of social expectations and thus "the adoption of society's view of themselves to the detriment of their freedom."[8] To stress pride as the fundamental human sin (and self-sacrifice as the corresponding virtue) is to discourage the need for women to assert their dignity in the struggle against their oppressors. The marginalized, and thus women, need to recover just what Niebuhr rejects, as their own temptation is the *refusal* to challenge entrenched power, not its proud disposition.

Niebuhr did not have a raised consciousness about the oppression of women, nor a developed sense of the need for the move-

7. Judith Plaskow, *Sex, Sin, and Grace: Women's Experience and the Theologies of Reinhold Niebuhr and Paul Tillich* (Lanham, Md.: University Press of America, 1980). See also Valerie Saiving Goldstein, "The Human Situation: A Feminine View," *Journal of Religion* 40 (April 1960): 100-112.

8. Plaskow, *Sex, Sin, and Grace,* 64.

ment that contemporary feminism rightly represents. However, hints of such sensitivity can be found in his comments on the importance of standards of justice within family life to protect women and children from the abuses of male power. Further, Niebuhr's understanding of the structure of human nature and its temptations is an anthropology that would put him in natural alliance with the struggle of women against systems of oppression, a predictable sequel to his support of the labor movement as a countervailing power to industrial autocracy. Indeed, there is a certain irony in the feminist critique of Niebuhr, for its employment of a hermeneutic of suspicion is kindred to his own wariness of both the corruptibility of power and its ideological justification.

A Niebuhrian response to feminist critics might go something like this:

1. Antecendent to any expression of sin is a primal human egocentricity, *coram deo* — "idolatry," variously described as "playing God" (Gen. 3:4-5), "self-deification," "unbelief," etc. As noted earlier, Niebuhr used the word "pride" to describe this basal incurvature: the placing of the self at the center of its universe and thus displacing the only One who belongs there. While a description of primordial self-centeredness as "pride" is misleading, especially when the word is used in his second sense as the sin of the powerful, it points to a universal self-regarding tendency which critics like Plaskow also acknowledge, even as they reconceptualize the *form* it takes in women's experience in this culture.

2. Sin, so understood as a universal predisposition, comes to expression in relations with others according to the distribution of power in a given historical context. Those with power — political, social, intellectual, moral, spiritual, etc. — manifest the self-serving propensity in terms of the corruption of the

power they possess, and thus as arrogance or *superbia* — "pride" in Niebuhr's second sense of the word. Those *without* power express primal sin as the refusal to risk its legitimate assertion, denying their claim to freedom as made in the image of God, and sinking into apathy or *acedia*. Niebuhr's description of the latter as "sensuality" tends to suggest the sins of the flesh and thus does not do justice to the wider understanding of it as the "escape from freedom" intended by the finitude/freedom symmetry of his doctrine of human nature, one that is in full conformity with Plaskow's concern. Further, a feminist hermeneutic of suspicion regarding legal, philosophical, political, religious, and other justifications of entrenched power is in exact continuity with Niebuhr's warnings about the self-righteous legitimation of vested interest — economic, political, social, moral, religious.

3. The Niebuhrian response to a feminist critique would not only call for a recognition of the similarities of analysis and a fairer representation of his position — with an admission of the ambiguity of his language and exposition — but also a counter-question about the ubiquity of sin, one presupposed by Plaskow and implied by others. Is there a consistent acknowledgment that sin affects the "champions of justice" as well as its "foes"? The polemic of feminist theology against patriarchy, including the tracing of all human suffering to androcentric theory and practice, appears to divide the world up too simplistically into the legions of light and the armies of night, with all the attendant dangers of self-righteous fury. A Manichaean reading of the struggle for justice ill serves that cause, for it provides no principle of internal self-criticism for its own legions, and no preparation for the temptations that come even to the powerless when their cause succeeds and they acquire the power so long and wrongly denied to them.

Religious Pluralism

While a common thread can be detected in all the foregoing -isms — a too sanguine reading of the human condition or parts thereof — the phenomenon of religious pluralism is a subject in its own right. Niebuhr did not expend great energies on pluralism as such, but he had some strong convictions about Judaism. These hint at implications for this important current topic. Also, his use of the concept "myth" might suggest similarities to current pluralist theologies that call into question the historic Christian assertion of the "scandal of particularity." In both of these cases, Niebuhr's thought anticipates current issues of pluralism and sheds light upon them.

A raised awareness of religious diversity and the pluralist theologies that have arisen in reponse to it (John Hick, Paul Knitter, etc.) pose fundamental questions about classical Christian teaching. Can we claim that Jesus Christ is unique, indeed that he is "the way, the truth, and the life" (John 14:6)? Must we not abandon the belief in the singular deity of Christ with its exclusivist and imperial connotations? Are devotees of other faiths and high religions, or people of commendable moral conduct, not as acceptable to God as Christian believers?

Niebuhr did not attend in depth to these questions. However, a much-commented-upon opinion of the later Niebuhr that Christians should not attempt to convert faithful Jews has implications for present Jewish-Christian theological questions. It also invites consideration of their import for the wider issues of religious pluralism.

"Antisupersessionism" — the belief that the coming of God in Jesus Christ does not abrogate the covenant with the Jewish people (Rom. 11:29) — is an increasingly widespread contention in ecumenical Christian circles. Niebuhr's position on proselytism seems to anticipate the antisupersessionist perspective found now in the statements of denominational assemblies and beyond.[9] Antisupersessionism, however, comes in many varieties. Niebuhr's version will have implications for his relation to the larger questions of religious pluralism.

Niebuhr's frequent alliances on social and political issues with Jewish compatriots confirmed his belief in the importance of the prophetic heritage of "biblical religion." The horror of the Holocaust and his strong support for establishing the state of Israel as an act of penitence and safe haven for Jews were yet other factors in this collegiality. These historical considerations, added to his honoring of the biblical faith of Jewish believers, laid the groundwork for his "no conversion" opinion. However, Niebuhr never repudiated the revelatory claims of Christian faith to the singular and surpassing disclosure of God in the person and work of Christ.[10] Thus he made a distinction, now common in the supersessionist debates, between the definitiveness of *noetic* claims for Christian revelation based on the decisive deed of God in Jesus Christ, but the "application of the benefits" of Christ's atoning work to others who do not confess Christ, and thus the extension of *soteric* claims to those with the justifying faith of Abraham (Rom. 4:9), then and now.[11] With Niebuhr's disinclination to ponder the fine points of systematic theology, it is unlikely that he would methodically pursue the

9. World Council of Churches, *The Theology of the Churches and the Jewish People: Statements by the World Council of Churches and Its Member Churches* (Geneva: WCC Publications, 1988).

10. See the essays of Paul Lehmann and William John Wolf in *Reinhold Niebuhr: His Religious, Social and Political Thought,* ed. Charles W. Kegley (New York: The Pilgrim Press, 1984), for astute analyses of Niebuhr's Christological and soteriological commitments. The first edition of this work was edited by Charles W. Kegley and Robert W. Bretall and published by Macmillan Company in 1956.

11. See Lehmann and Wolf in Kegley, ed., *Reinhold Niebuhr.*

intricacies of the current debate. However, his commitment to salvation by the grace of Abrahamic faith together with his belief in the definitiveness of God's disclosure in Christ move in the direction of this latter version of an antisupersessionism, one that preserves the particularity of the decisive deed and disclosure of redemption in Jesus Christ.[12]

Another kind of antisupersessionism makes similar assertions about the continuing covenant with, and legitimacy of, Jewish belief, but does so because all religious commitments are understood as varied historical and symbolic expressions of a common human experience of the holy, the good, etc. In this "experiential-expressivist" view of religious pluralism,[13] both the truth (ontological) and knowledge (revelatory) claims of Jewish and Christian faiths are denied. Particular religions are simply the historically shaped symbol systems for common-core sensibilities. Niebuhr's disquisitions on "myth" could be interpreted in this way. And, connected with his expressed views on the validity of Judaism, they might suggest that all high religions and people of good conscience would be assigned ontological and revelatory equivalency.

While a student at the University of Chicago in the midst of the then-current neonaturalism of Henry Nelson Wieman, I puzzled over an early version of this question. Was Niebuhr's belief in a "personal God" a poetic formulation, a "symbol," a "myth," needed by our affective nature to put us in touch with

12. For a survey of points of view in supersessionist/antisupersessionist debates and an argument for the eschatological position referred to in the text, see the writer's "The Place of Israel in Christian Faith," in *Gott lieben und seine Gebot halten,* Herausgegeben von Markus Bockmuehl und Helmut Burkhardt (Giessen/Basel: Brunnen-Verlag, 1991), 21-38.

13. The description is George Lindbeck's in his important work, *The Nature of Doctrine* (Philadelphia: Westminster Press, 1984).

the creative processes or depth dimension of the universe? Or did we have to do with Another? Thesis research on Niebuhr's categories showed that his use of "myth" and "symbol" carried both subjective and objective weight. In the words of the language philosopher Wilbur Urban, Niebuhr held that Christian symbols entailed both "symbolic truth" — evocative and expressive power — and also the "truth of the symbol" — reliable reference to ultimate Reality. For Niebuhr, the God we address in prayer and confront in the heights and depths of human history is the One with whom we have to do.

Niebuhr's assertions about the beginning, middle, and end of history, while couched in the biblical language and cosmology of a pre-scientific age, do refer to real events done and to be done by a real God. Since this is so, Niebuhr's "biblical theology" presupposes the singular deeds and disclosures of God in Israel and Christ with no equivalency in other religions, a position that would put his views on particularity in conflict with the relativism of today's pluralist theologies.

The linkage of relativist theologies to the visionary perspectives discussed throughout this work lies in the pluralist presupposition that the human condition needs no special divine acts of redemption or revelation. Universal humanity is endowed with capacities for knowing and doing the truth. A certain Benevolence gives access under the many names of world religions or through the good dispositions of a humane conscience and behavior.

Niebuhr's concept of "general revelation" served him well in the ethical analysis that argued in the public forum for the illuminative power of biblical anthropology. It has implications for the present subject. A belief in general revelation holds that enough of the *imago Dei* survives, by a common grace, so that traces of the divine presence and purpose and norms for life together are universally discernible in the high religions and in people of conscience. So Niebuhr could, and did, acknowledge the presence and power of God at work well beyond the perimeters of Christian faith. Within Niebuhr's framework of biblical drama, we might say that these "little lights" (Barth) are given so that the story might go forward. So understood, Niebuhr would be (and was) an advocate of dialogue well beyond the Jewish-Christian family of faith, and could even acknowledge a catalytic role for other religions in that encounter, one that would remind Christian believers of forgotten riches in their own tradition.

Because Niebuhr's theology is biblical-dramatic, it includes the distinct and different deed of God in the election of Israel and, definitively, the central act of disclosure and deliverance in the life, death, and resurrection of Jesus Christ. The reason these divine deeds are necessary is that human history is not, finally, self-redeeming and self-disclosing. Human nature is too captive to its own agendas to assume that it can find its own way to ultimate truth or make its way to ultimate salvation by its moral or spiritual practices. The deeds of *special* revelation and redemption are part and parcel of the biblical drama. It is hard to imagine a Niebuhr not as eager to share these historical specifics about ultimate matters as he was to set forth biblical distinctives in his social, political, and economic commentary on penultimate concerns.

Limitations and Conclusions

If theological durability over yet another twenty-three years is evidence, then Martin Marty's editorial expectations in his 1970 "Promise" series were accurate — at least regarding one of the theologians in that number, Reinhold Niebuhr. Not only have his political wisdom and ethical insights lived on, but their theological framework continues to be timely. Indeed, the short memory of today's visionaries about the exposure of yesterday's illusions makes understandable the cry now heard here and there, "Reinhold Niebuhr, where are you when we need you?"

Stressed in this update chapter have been the strengths of Niebuhr's thought that have given it staying power. But there are weaknesses as well. A theologian who calls ever and again for the self-critical spirit must live under that same mandate. Niebuhr gave evidence of that readiness for self-examination in his response to critics in the notable volume on his work in the Library of Living Theology.[14] And, as earlier noted, the leading theme of June Bingham's biography of Niebuhr is "the courage to change." What are some of the limitations of his theology in equipping us for questions faced at the close of this century?

Niebuhr did little to prepare us for relationships with a self-critical and ecumenical evangelicalism. Like too much mainline and academic commentary, in his time and currently as well, he had little grasp of the diversity within evangelical ranks, the quality of its scholarship, and the justice and peace agenda of a significant minority of its constituents.[15] He tended to see in evangelicalism only a fundamentalist reading of Scripture or an apolitical piety regularly seduced by the economic and political powers and principalities. Evangelicals often responded in kind, writing him off as a closet liberal. The convergences of his biblical theology with evangelical essentials may now be discernible more clearly as the smoke of former battles clears.

14. Kegley and Bretall, eds., *Reinhold Niebuhr.*

15. For the meaning of "evangelical" as used in this context, see the writer's entry, "Evangelical, Evangelicalism," in *Westminster Dictionary of Christian Theology,* ed. Alan Richardson and John Bowden (Philadelphia: Westminster Press, 1983), 191-92, and *Ecumenical Faith in Evangelical Perspective* (Grand Rapids: Eerdmans Publishing Co., 1993), *passim.*

As noted before, aspects of his thought that might have given support to the struggle of women were muted. William Wolf early detected that the importance of self-affirmation by those tempted to "escape from freedom" was left undeveloped by Niebuhr because of his preoccupation with "pride" (called Pride 2 here).[16] This omission made his work less accessible to feminists, and in fact, made him a prime target for their critique of androcentric thought.

A common criticism of Niebuhr's theology is its unsystematic nature, giving too little attention to one or another of the classical loci, and/or their interrelationships: Trinity, person of Christ, doctrine of the church, sacraments and ministry, etc. Niebuhr acknowledged the legitimacy of the charge, with apologies for being only an ethicist or preacher. The irony is that his thought has had far greater impact on the theology of the twentieth century than ideas of most self-identified "theologians." However, the current outpouring of major systematic works that seek to cover all the topics is a sign of the Christian community's need to recover its full story in the face of the competing ideologies of the age. Niebuhr like Luther was "an irregular theologian," necessary to light the fires of renewal and reform. Others are required to feed and tend them.

Those of us warmed by the fires lit by the Niebuhr of another day can only wish that their embers may yet bring new flame.

16. William John Wolf, "Reinhold Niebuhr's Doctrine of Man," in Kegley, ed., *Reinhold Niebuhr*, 317.

chapter 7

TALL TALES ABOUT
REINHOLD NIEBUHR

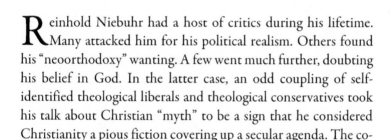

R einhold Niebuhr had a host of critics during his lifetime. Many attacked him for his political realism. Others found his "neoorthodoxy" wanting. A few went much further, doubting his belief in God. In the latter case, an odd coupling of self-identified theological liberals and theological conservatives took his talk about Christian "myth" to be a sign that he considered Christianity a pious fiction covering up a secular agenda. The coterie of Harvard faculty that whimsically described itself as "atheists for Niebuhr" seemed to give credence to the charge.

Tall Tale 1: Niebuhr Was Not a Christian

Suspicions about Niebuhr's ultimate commitments resurfaced in Stanley Hauerwas's recent Gifford Lectures.[1] There Hauerwas

1. Stanley Hauerwas, *With the Grain of the Universe: The Church's Witness and Natural Theology* (Grand Rapids: Brazos Press, 2001).

This chapter first appeared as "Was Reinhold Niebuhr a Christian?" in *First Things,* Number 126, October 2002. Reprinted by permission.

asks, "Do we have anything more in Niebuhr than a complex humanism disguised in the language of the Christian faith?" For Hauerwas, "It is hard to think that Niebuhr's God is anything more or less than an unavoidable aspect of our consciousness."[2] Which leads Hauerwas to wonder: Is Niebuhr's theology, at bottom, merely a "naturalistic view of the world," the worship of "a domesticated god capable of doing no more than providing comfort to the anxious conscience of the bourgeoisie"?[3] In fact, the rejection of both humanism and naturalism is a constant from Niebuhr's early liberal period, when he argued in the 1927 *Does Civilization Need Religion?* against both the religious depersonalization of the universe and the political and economic depersonalization of society, to his post-liberal two-volume classic, *The Nature and Destiny of Man,* and beyond, where he casts the issue in Christian-specific terms. Telling examples of the latter can be found in his 1956 comments on the religious naturalism of Henry Nelson Wieman:

> The trouble with religious naturalism is not only that it obscures the whole mystery of the divine, the mystery of creativity and grace, but that it also falsifies the whole drama of human history. . . . Professor Wieman is under the impression that a classical Christian faith is merely a crude, prescientific way of looking at the world, God, and the self. . . . The only trouble with this picture is that all significant truths and facts about man and God, about the nobility and misery of human freedom, and about the judgment and mercy of God, are left out of the picture.[4]

2. Hauerwas, *With the Grain of the Universe,* 131, 130.

3. Hauerwas, *With the Grain of the Universe,* 138.

4. Charles W. Kegley and Robert W. Bretall, eds., *Reinhold Niebuhr: His Religious, Social, and Political Thought,* Library of Living Theology, vol. 2 (New

Likewise, in response to Paul Tillich's charge of "supernatural-ism," Niebuhr wrote:

> I do not believe that ontological categories can do justice to the freedom either of the divine or the human person, or to . . . the forgiveness by God of man's sin. . . . If it is "supernaturalistic" to affirm that faith discerns the key to specific meaning above the categories of philosophy, ontological or epistemological, then I must plead guilty of being a supernaturalist. The whole of the Bible is an exposition of this kind of supernaturalism. If we are embarrassed by this and try to interpret biblical religion in other terms, we end in changing the very character of Christian faith.[5]

Tall Tale 2: Niebuhr Did Not Pray

Germane to the question of a Niebuhrian "naturalistic view of the world" is his prayer life. Judging her husband's prayers to be key to his faith, Ursula Niebuhr assembled a representative collection of them in *Justice and Mercy*,[6] along with some of the sermons from his decades of circuit-riding in college and seminary chapels. She introduces his prayers with his own outline of a biblical sequencing to be observed by the "priestly function" of a pastor: "praise and thanksgiving . . . humility and contrition . . . intercession . . . aspiration."[7] All such prayer is directed to "the

---

York: Macmillan, 1956) with an updated and enlarged edition edited by Charles Kegley (New York: Pilgrim Press, 1984), 524-25. The citation here is from the latter, as also are other references from the Kegley volume.

5. Quoted in Kegley, ed., *Reinhold Niebuhr*, 509.

6. Ursula Niebuhr, *Justice and Mercy* (San Francisco: Harper & Row, 1974).

7. Ursula Niebuhr, *Justice and Mercy*, 2, 3, 4.

divine person" of whom he reminds Wieman and Tillich. Among the most memorable prayers is the "serenity prayer" that was circulated among soldiers in World War II by the USO and incorporated by Alcoholics Anonymous and others into their twelve-step programs. The prayer comes in various formulations, of which the most common is "God grant me the serenity to accept the things I cannot change, the courage to change the things I can, and the wisdom to know the difference."

Tall Tale 3: Niebuhr Held a "Low" Christology

What about Niebuhr's teaching on such central Christian convictions as the Incarnation and the Atonement? According to Hauerwas, it lacks "high Christology" and offers only "'the ethics of Jesus' without the need to engage in any further Christological claims."[8] But Paul Lehmann, who has done an extensive study of the "Christological claims" of his Union Seminary colleague, concludes that "Christology has been and is the principal passion and purpose of his theological work . . . the leitmotiv of Niebuhr's theology. . . . Christology is *pivotal*, not *peripheral* . . . a remarkably evangelical view of the person and work of Jesus Christ."[9]

Niebuhr himself thanked Lehmann for his "account of the centrality of my Christological interest and the development of my thought in the direction of a more adequate Christology than the older liberalism with which I began."[10] Thus the Atonement wrought on the Cross, with the Incarnation as premise, is "the good news of the Gospel . . . that God takes the sinfulness of man

---

8. Hauerwas, *With the Grain of the Universe*, 99.
9. Kegley, ed., *Reinhold Niebuhr*, 329, 331, 351, 339.
10. Kegley, ed., *Reinhold Niebuhr*, 514-15.

into Himself and overcomes in His own heart what cannot be overcome in human life."[11]

Tall Tale 4: Niebuhr Thought the Biblical Narratives Were Myth

Interestingly, Niebuhr deals with this paradox of divine suffering with a profundity that anticipates the current debate on divine impassibility[12] when he writes,

> Christian orthodoxy has been rightly afraid of a too consistent emphasis upon the suffering of God. It has declared the doctrine that God the Father suffers to be a heresy (the heresy of "patripassionism"). Yet it has affirmed that God the Son suffers and that the Father and the Son are One. To insist on the distinction between the majesty of the Father and the suffering of the Son, and yet to declare that the Father and the Son are one, is an effort to state, within the limits of human understanding, our comprehension and lack of comprehension of a form of peace which passeth understanding. If the suffering of God is emphasized too completely we arrive at the heretical conception of a finite God. . . . If the peace of God is defined too rationalistically . . . we arrive at a conception of a peace which is purchased at the price of detachment.[13]

11. Reinhold Niebuhr, *The Nature and Destiny of Man*, vol. 1 (New York: Charles Scribner's Sons, 1945), 142.

12. As in Thomas Weinandy, "Does God Suffer?" *First Things*, Number 116, November 2001.

13. Reinhold Niebuhr, "The Peace of God," in *Discerning the Signs of the Times* (New York: Charles Scribner's Sons, 1946), 183.

But can't such passages simply be dismissed as myth-mongering? It was such a question that led Niebuhr to modify his language by 1956. "The word ['myth'] has subjective and skeptical connotations. I am sorry I ever used it, particularly since the project for 'demythologizing' the Bible has been undertaken and bids fair to reduce the Biblical revelation to eternally valid truths without any existential encounters between God and man."[14] That said, Niebuhr's attempt to describe key points in the biblical macro-narrative — from creation and fall, through virginal conception and resurrection to history's finale — as "permanent myths" can also be interpreted in light of current investigations of metaphor, story, and symbol as apt ways of speaking about who God is and what God does. Neither are they very far removed from Karl Barth's assertion that a "divinatory imagination" is at work in the making of biblical "sagas."

Tall Tale 5: Niebuhr Did Not Believe in the Resurrection

Take, for instance, Niebuhr on the eschaton. Using a distinction found in the work of the philosopher of language Wilbur Urban, we can say that Niebuhr viewed the eschatology of the Book of Revelation as an evocative "symbolic truth," at the center of which is "the truth of the symbol." In his academic rendering of this truth in *The Nature and Destiny of Man*, Niebuhr asserts his belief that history has a definite "End," in the sense both of conclusion and goal. In sermonic settings — from Easter message to burial homily — he proclaimed the final victory of Christ over death in the language of "the resurrection of the body":

14. Niebuhr, "Reply to Interpretation and Criticism," in Kegley and Bretall, eds., *Reinhold Niebuhr*, 439.

Some of us have been persuaded to take the stone which we then rejected and to make it the head of the corner. . . . There is no part of the Apostolic Creed which . . . expresses the whole genius of the Christian faith more neatly than just that despised phrase, "I believe in the resurrection of the body."[15]

Niebuhr has often been taken to task for saying that he understands such terms "seriously, but not literally." But he intended such comments as expressions of modesty, since we are incapable in our finitude of describing the "furniture of heaven and the temperature of hell." Yet Niebuhr wrote that while "it is . . . important to maintain a decent measure of restraint; . . . it is equally important not to confuse restraint with uncertainty about the validity of hope that 'when he shall appear, we shall be like him; for we shall see him as he is' (1 John 3:2)."[16] He elaborates further on the mysteries of our resurrection in poignant 1967 remarks on his approaching death. Niebuhr's minimalist description of our final destiny might not be sufficient for the concluding chapter of a textbook in systematic theology, but it is outrageous to deny that this ethicist and unsystematic theologian did not hold to core biblical testimony about the world to come.

Tall Tale 6: Niebuhr Did Not Have a Clear Understanding of the Church

Critics often accuse Niebuhr of lacking an ecclesiology. As a pastor and teacher in the church he helped to found, the Evangelical

15. Reinhold Niebuhr, *Beyond Tragedy* (New York: Charles Scribner's Sons, 1937), 289-90.
16. Reinhold Niebuhr, *The Nature and Destiny of Man,* vol. 2 (New York: Charles Scribner's Sons, 1945), 298.

and Reformed Church, I saw for myself his deep immersion in and love for the church. This ecclesial context is basic to who he was and how he thought, especially so his shaping by both the Reformed and Lutheran traditions of his church. While Niebuhr never attempted to construct a systematic ecclesiology, his life and faith cannot be understood without a grasp of the functional ecclesiology in which they are grounded.

Fierce attacks on a theologian long gone are testimony to that theologian's durability. The new edition of Charles Brown's insightful study *Niebuhr and His Age* (2002) and Langdon Gilkey's *On Niebuhr: A Theological Study* (2001) both effectively refute his harshest critics and in doing so contribute to a Niebuhr renaissance prompted at least in part by the misreadings of others.

As June Bingham noted in the title of her thoughtful biography, *Courage to Change* (1993), Niebuhr was always willing to reconsider his earlier positions. But this should not distract from his perduring affirmation of Christian centralities. Indeed, those who remember him as a pastor and knew him as a theologian do not doubt that Niebuhr's "courage to change" rose from an abiding serenity of faith in the One to whom he prayed and about whom he faithfully preached and taught.

A Selected Bibliography of Works by Reinhold Niebuhr

Does Civilization Need Religion? A Study in the Social Resources and Limitations of Religion in Modern Life. New York: The Macmillan Company, 1927, 1941.

Leaves from the Notebook of a Tamed Cynic. New York: Willet, Clark and Colby, 1929; World Publishing Company (Meridian Books), 1957; San Francisco: Harper & Row, 1980; Louisville: Westminster/John Knox, 1990.

The Contribution of Religion to Social Work. New York: Columbia University Press, 1932.

Moral Man and Immoral Society. New York: Charles Scribner's Sons, 1932, 1960. Also published in Japanese and Korean translations.

Reflections on the End of an Era. New York: Charles Scribner's Sons, 1934.

An Interpretation of Christian Ethics. New York: Harper & Brothers, 1935; World Publishing Company (Meridian Books), 1956, with a new preface by the author, 1963; San Francisco: Harper & Row, 1986. Also published in Japanese translation.

Beyond Tragedy: Essays on the Christian Interpretation of History. New York: Charles Scribner's Sons, 1937; New York: The Macmillan Company, 1979. Also published in German and Polish translations.

Christianity and Power Politics. New York: Charles Scribner's Sons, 1940; Archon, Shoe String Press, 1969.

Why the Christian Church Is Not Pacifist. London: Student Christian Movement Press, 1940.

The Nature and Destiny of Man: A Christian Interpretation. Vol. 1, *Human Nature.* New York: Charles Scribner's Sons, 1941. Vol. 2, *Human Destiny.* 1943; one-volume edition, 1948, 1953, 1964. Also published in German, French, Dutch, Japanese, and Chinese translations.

The Children of Light and the Children of Darkness: A Vindication of Democracy and a Critique of Its Traditional Defense. New York: Charles Scribner's Sons, 1944; New York: The Macmillan Company, 1977. Also published in German, Dutch, Czech, and Japanese translations.

The Contribution of Religion to Cultural Unity. Haddam, Conn.: The Edward Hazen Foundation, 1945.

Discerning the Signs of the Times: Sermons for Today and Tomorrow. New York: Charles Scribner's Sons, 1946. Also published in German, Dutch, and Czech translations.

Faith and History: A Comparison of Christian and Modern Views of History. New York: Charles Scribner's Sons, 1949; New York: The Macmillan Company, 1977. Also published in German, French, Swedish, and Japanese translations.

The Irony of American History. New York: Charles Scribner's Sons, 1952, 1958; New York: The Macmillan Company, 1982. Also published in French, Spanish, and Japanese translations.

Christian Realism and Political Problems. New York: Charles Scribner's Sons, 1953; New York: Kelley, 1977.

The Self and the Dramas of History. New York: Charles Scribner's Sons, 1955. Also published in Japanese translation.

Love and Justice: Selections from the Shorter Writings of Reinhold Niebuhr. Edited with an introduction by D. B. Robertson. Philadelphia: Westminster Press, 1957; Cleveland: World Publishing Company (Meridian Books), 1967; Louisville: Westminster/John Knox, 1992.

The World Crisis and American Responsibility: Nine Essays. Edited with an introduction by Ernest W. Lefever. New York: Association Press, 1958; Westport, Conn.: Greenwood, 1974.

Pious and Secular America. New York: Charles Scribner's Sons, 1958. Also published in German translation.

Essays in Applied Christianity. Selected and edited with an introduction by D. B. Robertson. New York: World Publishing Company (Meridian Books), 1959.

The Structure of Nations and Empires: A Study of Recurring Patterns and Problems of the Political Order in Relation to the Unique Problems of the Nuclear Age. New York: Charles Scribner's Sons, 1959; New York: Kelley, 1977. Also published in German translation.

Reinhold Niebuhr on Politics: His Political Philosophy and Its Application to Our Age as Expressed in His Writings. Edited with an introduction by Harry R. Davis and Robert C. Good. New York: Charles Scribner's Sons, 1960.

A Nation So Conceived: Reflections on the History of America from Its Early Visions to Its Present Power. With Alan Heimert. New York: Charles Scribner's Sons, 1963.

Man's Nature and His Communities: Essays on the Dynamics and Enigmas of Man's Personal and Social Existence. New York: Charles Scribner's Sons, 1965, 1968; Lanham, Md.: University Press of America, 1988. Also published in Japanese translation.

Faith and Politics: A Commentary on Religious, Social and Political Thought in a Technological Age. Edited with an introduction by Ronald H. Stone. New York: George Braziller, 1968.

The Democratic Experience: Past and Prospects. With Paul E. Sigmund. New York: Praeger Publishers, 1969.

Justice and Mercy [sermons and prayers]. Edited with an introduction by Ursula M. Niebuhr. New York: Harper & Row, 1974; Louisville: Westminster/John Knox Press, 1991.

Young Reinhold Niebuhr: His Early Writings, 1911-1931. Edited with an introduction by William G. Chrystal. St. Louis: Eden Publishing House, 1977.

The Essential Reinhold Niebuhr: Selected Essays and Addresses. Edited with an introduction by Robert McAfee Brown. New Haven: Yale University Press, 1986.

Reinhold Niebuhr: Theologian of Public Life. Edited with an introduction by Larry Rasmussen. London: Collins, 1989; Minneapolis: Augsburg Fortress Press, 1991.

Reinhold Niebuhr Reader: Selected Essays, Articles, and Book Reviews. Edited with an introduction by Charles C. Brown. Philadelphia: Trinity Press International, 1992.

Other Books by Gabriel Fackre

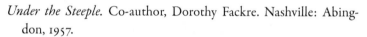

Under the Steeple. Co-author, Dorothy Fackre. Nashville: Abingdon, 1957.

The Purpose and Work of the Ministry. Philadelphia: Christian Education Press, 1959.

The Pastor and the World. Philadelphia: United Church Press, 1964.

Conversation in Faith. Philadelphia: United Church Press, 1968.

Secular Impact. Philadelphia: Pilgrim Press, 1968.

The Rainbow Sign: Christian Futurity. London: Epworth, 1969. Grand Rapids: Eerdmans, 1969.

Humiliation and Celebration: Post-Radical Themes in Doctrine, Morals, and Mission. New York: Sheed and Ward, 1969.

Liberation in Middle America. Philadelphia: Pilgrim Press, 1968.

Do and Tell: Theological Themes in Evangelism. Grand Rapids: Eerdmans, 1973, 1974, 1975.

Word and Deed: Theological Themes in Evangelism. Grand Rapids: Eerdmans, 1975.

The Christian Story: A Narrative Interpretation of Basic Christian Doctrine. Grand Rapids: Eerdmans, 1978.

Youth Ministry: The Gospel and the People. Co-author, Jan Chartier. Philadelphia: Judson Press, 1979, 1980.

Other Books by Gabriel Fackre

The Religious Right and Christian Faith. Grand Rapids: Eerdmans, 1982, 1983.

The Christian Story. Vol. 1. Revised edition. Grand Rapids: Eerdmans, 1982, 1983.

The Christian Story: Scripture in the Church for the World. Vol. 2. Grand Rapids: Eerdmans, 1987.

Christian Basics: A Primer for Pilgrims. Co-author, Dorothy Fackre. Grand Rapids: Eerdmans, 1991, 1992, 1993.

Ecumenical Faith in Evangelical Perspective. Grand Rapids: Eerdmans, 1993.

What about Those Who Have Never Heard? Co-authors, Ronald Nash and John Sanders. Downers Grove: InterVarsity Press, 1995, 11th printing 2010.

The Doctrine of Revelation: A Narrative Interpretation. Edinburgh: Edinburgh University Press and Grand Rapids: Eerdmans, 1997. (Vol. 3, *The Christian Story: A Pastoral Systematics.*)

Restoring the Center: Essays Evangelical and Ecumenical. Downers Grove: InterVarsity Press, 1998.

Affirmations and Admonitions. Co-author, Michael Root. Grand Rapids: Eerdmans, 1998.

Judgment Day at the White House: Exploring Moral Issues and the Political Use and Abuse of Religion. Editor. Grand Rapids: Eerdmans, 1999.

The Day After: A Retrospective on Religious Dissent in the Presidential Crisis. Grand Rapids: Eerdmans, 2000.

Believing, Doing, and Caring in the United Church of Christ. Cleveland: United Church Press, 2005.

Christology in Context. (Vol. 4, *The Christian Story: A Pastoral Systematics.*) Grand Rapids: Eerdmans, 2006.

The Church: Signs of the Spirit and Signs of the Times. (Vol. 5, *The Christian Story: A Pastoral Systematics.*) Grand Rapids: Eerdmans, 2007.

About the Author and Contributors

———— ✇ ————

The author, Gabriel Fackre, is Abbot Professor Emeritus of Christian Theology at Andover Newton Theological School in Newton, Massachusetts, where he taught for twenty-five years. He began his ministry in Chicago and Pittsburgh, serving industrial parishes for twelve years. From 1961 to 1970 he taught theology at Lancaster Theological Seminary in Pennsylvania.

Dr. Fackre is the author of twenty-five books in the fields of theology and ethics and has served as president of the American Theological Society. A member of the United Church of Christ, he represented it in the Lutheran-Reformed Conversation, Jewish-Christian dialogue, and the Consultation on Church Union. He has taken an active part in grassroots theological renewal movements, including the co-founding of the Craigville Colloquies. He and his spouse, Dorothy, live on the grounds of the United Church of Christ center in Craigville, Massachusetts.

Martin E. Marty is the Fairfax M. Cone Distinguished Service Professor Emeritus at the University of Chicago, where he taught for thirty-five years. Among his many books are *The Mystery of the Child* and *Building Cultures of Trust.* He is a minister in the Evangelical Lutheran Church in America.

The late Daniel Novotny, along with his wife Jean, was an adjunct lecturer at Andover Newton Theological School. Both graduates of Union Seminary, New York, they served United Church of Christ parishes in New England and Alabama. For a decade they were the directors of a summer session at Mansfield College in Oxford University.